Forever Hellos,
Hard Good-Byes

Forever Hellos,
Hard Good-Byes

Inspiration, wit, & wisdom
from courageous kids facing
life-threatening illness

Axel Dahlberg
Janis Russell Love

free spirit
PUBLiSHiNG®

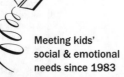

Meeting kids'
social & emotional
needs since 1983

Library of Congress Cataloging-in-Publication Data
Dahlberg, Axel.
  Forever hellos, hard good-byes : inspiration, wit & wisdom from courageous kids facing life-threatening illness / by Axel Dahlberg and Janis Russell Love.
     p. cm.
  ISBN-13: 978-1-57542-272-5
  ISBN-10: 1-57542-272-7
  1. Sick children—Psychology—Juvenile literature. 2. Chronically ill children—Psychology—Juvenile literature. I. Love, Janis Russell. II. Title.
  RJ47.5.D34 2007
  618.92—dc22

                                                                    2007035769

The authors are donating a portion of the proceeds from the sale of this book to charities through The Foundation of the Carolinas.

Edited by Al Desetta and John Kober
Cover design by Marieka Heinlen
Interior design by Natasha Keynon

10 9 8 7 6 5 4 3 2 1
Printed in the United States of America

Free Spirit Publishing Inc.
217 Fifth Avenue North, Suite 200
Minneapolis, MN 55401-1299
(612) 338-2068
help4kids@freespirit.com
www.freespirit.com

Free Spirit Publishing is a member of the Green Press Initiative, and we're committed to printing our books on recycled paper containing a minimum of 30% post-consumer waste (PCW). For every ton of books printed on 30% PCW recycled paper, we save 5.1 trees, 2,100 gallons of water, 114 gallons of oil, 18 pounds of air pollution, 1,230 kilowatt hours of energy, and .9 cubic yards of landfill space. At Free Spirit it's our goal to nurture not only young people, but nature too!

green press
INITIATIVE

Dedication

In loving memory of Scott Alan Russell

Acknowledgments

First, we have to thank all of the wonderful families who allowed us into their lives, and shared with us some of their most private moments and thoughts. Without the graciousness and openness of these families, this book never would have never been possible.

We would also like to thank David Williams, president and CEO of Make-A-Wish Foundation of America; Dr. Lori Wiener of the National Cancer Institute, National Institutes of Health; Senator Stephen J. Buoniconti of the Commonwealth of Massachusetts State Senate; Janet T. Fortner and Hospice & Palliative Care Charlotte Region; Pam Barrett, Meghan Davis, Marion Taylor, and Paul Russ and Kids Path Hospice & Palliative Care of Greensboro, North Carolina; Gina Volonte, Kathy Dolan, and Legacy Emanuel Children's Hospital in Portland, Oregon; Rebecca Baglio and Natrisha Bayer and the Valerie Fund Children's Center at Newark Beth Israel Medical Center in Newark, New Jersey; Dr. Robert Brooks, clinical psychologist; Lori Pearson, certified Child Life specialist and lecturer at Edgewood College; Nora Hager, Child Life program coordinator at the University of Missouri; Barbara Woodring and the Society of Pediatric Nurses; Jaydene and John Chandler; Kimberly Barker and the Children's Specialty Center at Carolinas Medical Center; Ester A. Scott of New Directions of Columbus County, North Carolina; Mike Formy-Duval; Randy Spencer; Frank and Brenda Hunter; Jack and Cathy Flynn of Tucat Studio; Mike Johnson; Terri Johnson; Kaye Yaffe; Misty Meadows Mitey Riders; the Swimmer family; Teresa White; Alan Smith; Alexis Burling; and Dylan Holmes.

We would also like to thank our agent, Roslyn Targ, and Free Spirit Publishing for believing in the voices of these children. Finally, we'd like to thank our friends and families who supported us throughout this project.

Contents

Preface viii

Introduction 1

Meet the Gang 2

Chapter 1: Finding Out 12

Chapter 2: Friends and Telling Friends 31

Chapter 3: Life—the Good, the Bad, and the Downright Ugly 42

Chapter 4: Adventures in School 66

Chapter 5: Hospital Tips and Tales 83

Chapter 6: Family Fun and Fuss 108

Chapter 7: Dealing with Our Public 123

Chapter 8: Special Memories and Special Friends 142

Chapter 9: I Can Do Anything You Can Do 154

Chapter 10: Back at You 162

Chapter 11: Advice and Wisdom—Never Give Up 176

Epilogue 192

Glossary of Medical Terms 198

About the Authors 205

Preface

Writing this book proved to be a tremendous spiritual journey that changed our lives forever. More than simply taking stock of our own lives and no longer worrying about bad hair days, we were reminded how delightful the human spirit is, and how beautiful life is when viewed through the eyes of kids.

We started the book four years ago when we discovered there were no books available for kids with life-threatening and life-altering diseases. Sure, there were books that told the story of one child's illness or how to cope with the severe illness or death of a loved one or pet. But no books were written for the kids themselves—no words of compassion, wisdom, or advice from kids who had gone before. Nearly all of the existing books on this topic were written by the parent of an ill child who shared only his or her child's story, or by doctors and scholars in a vocabulary that was nearly impossible to understand. These books may have included quotes from kids, but the quotes were often used to tell a larger story or to argue a larger point. We believe nothing is **larger** than the words of kids talking honestly and openly to other kids.

It's taken us four years to write this book, because our biggest hurdle was getting access to kids with severe health issues. Understandably, parents and guardians of very ill kids are quite protective during these stressful and scary times. Add the increasingly strict health privacy laws and the task, we discovered well into the process, seemed insurmountable. But we persisted, even though months would pass between interviewing kids. Once we gained the trust of some of the families and organizations, we began to get referrals. Gradually, our network of kids began to stretch from coast to coast.

These wonderful children and teens opened up to us, sometimes slowly, sometimes immediately. In all of the interviews, we shared heart-stopping emotions, but we knew that we could not cry first, if it came to that (and there were moments when it did). We could shed tears *with* the families, never *before* them. We had no idea how difficult it would be to hear some of these stories. Conversely, there were times when we had tears in our eyes from laughing so hard.

Parents or friends were always present during the interviews. The parents helped by prompting memories in the child, or filling in background information. Often, parents told us they had never heard such thoughts from their own child.

People ask us what we learned from this process. One thing that stands out is all of the misdiagnoses the kids endured. We urge families and children to press their doctors and nurses to make certain that little aches really are just sore muscles or sprains. Odds are it is nothing; but it is important to be sure. The other thing we learned is how cruel and inhospitable our society can be for anyone who seems different. We know kids can be brutally cruel. But the thoughtless looks and comments these kids have heard from adults are unbelievable.

These wonderful kids and their families graciously allowing us into their lives and sharing with us some of their most private and painful moments is what kept us going. These families needed to know that their time and energy was not in vain. Sharing their experiences with, and offering guidance to, others somehow made their journeys make *some* sense. The kids trusted us—strangers—with their stories in the hopes that those close to them, and those far away, would hear the truth deep in their hearts and would find strength through their words.

Axel Dahlberg & Janis Russell Love

Introduction

The 34 kids whose voices are in this book, ranging from ages 6 to 22, have dealt with realities—including death—that few of us can comprehend. Wise beyond their years, you cannot shhh . . . these kids.

> "Well kids want to be treated special; ill kids want to be treated *normal.*"

From all across the nation and all socioeconomic groups, these kids face a variety of life-threatening and/or life-altering illnesses. They selected the topics for discussion—what *they* deemed important. They share stories of discovery and their thoughts about death and dying; their families, friends, teachers, and medical professionals who have become part of their lives; their treatments, physical pain, and emotional drain; their anger, sadness, laughter, stumbles, hopes, desires, and pranks; how they are treated and want to be treated; and how friends and strangers have given to them, and how they have given back. The driving force behind the book is their remarkable and captivating words that entertain and encourage, and offer insight, inspiration, and knowledge.

The kids have three things in common: 1) Circumstances that will forever alter their lives, 2) an overwhelming desire to be heard, and 3) a universal wish to be treated "normal." They don't want pity—they want respect and understanding, even friendliness in public places. In a time of increasing awareness and diversity, we need to extend this loving community to kids who are *perceived* as different.

In addition to tears, sorrow, and crises, their stories also include laugh-out-loud humor. This book captures the entirety of the kids' experiences—laughter, tears, boredom, excitement—everything you'd expect to find when kids are involved in any situation. This is not a book of doom and gloom. It is a book about *real* kids with *real* personalities, who are trying to make the best of times during the worst of times.

The two of us as authors, all the kids and their gracious families, the doctors, nurses, social workers, Child Life specialists, and the many wonderful people who had a part in making this book a reality hope that you will find comfort, guidance, and moments that touch you—that you relate to, that make you laugh, and that bring kinship with these remarkable kids. We hope that through them you might better understand yourself and your own situation and experiences. Whether you are a child facing what seems dark and dreary, a parent, a medical or social professional, or any number of family members, friends, or interested parties who interact with children, we hope the voices of these children inspire you.

Meet the Gang

Justin, 6

I have hemophilia, which means that my blood does not clot properly. So, if I'm bleeding, it doesn't stop as quickly as other people. I've never had a bleed that we couldn't stop. It's a disease that you can get from your parents. My brother has it, too. Other than getting shots, our days are just about the same as other boys. We think our lives are pretty normal. We run around and play, fall down, and then get right back up. I've been playing the piano since I was four. I'm on the swim team. I can even dive and do flips. Hemophilia is just something that I've always had. I really don't think anything of it. I want people to know that my life is pretty normal, and I'm funny.

Cassidy, 7

I was born without any eyes or a nose. I have to breathe through my mouth. I have prosthetic (which means "fake") eyes. There are advantages to being blind, like no one can ever sneak up on me because I hear so well, and I can't see other people staring at me if I make a scene in public. I can see; I just see differently. But I don't have to do anything differently in my life (okay, except I walk with a cane for blind people). I've been playing the piano since I was three. I also play golf—yeah, golf! I'm not afraid of anything—okay, thunderstorms scare me.

Matthew, 9

I was born with hemophilia. My brother also has hemophilia, but we have never really had anything serious happen. I'm pretty much like any other kid. I swim, play baseball, and I play the piano. The only difference, I guess, is that I've written two books, *My Brother Is Getting a New Port* and *If You Wear a Medic Alert*. I don't like to talk about my hemophilia, like my brother does. I want people to treat me normal and not ask me questions.

> "We don't dwell on the problem, we focus on a solution."
> —*Jonathan*

> "I'm not blind, I just see differently."
> —*Cassidy*

> "If they ever offer you anything, always ask for a dog." —*Scotty*

2

Kimberlie, 10

I have acute lymphoblastic leukemia, also called ALL. It's cancer in my blood and a very serious illness. I live with my mom, dad, big sister Stephanie, our dogs Mocha and Buttercup, and two fish named Hope and Faith. I am energetic and happy, and some of my favorite things to do are play soccer, basketball, hang out with my family and friends, play soccer, work on my scrapbook, play soccer, read, write (Did I mention that I like to play soccer?), go to school, oh, and play soccer. Being interviewed for this book was very difficult for me because it brought back many painful memories, but I wanted to do it to help other kids.

Lindsey, 10

I'm in the fifth grade, and I have spina bifida, which means that part of my spinal cord is exposed inside my body. My legs and lower body functions are affected, so I mostly use a wheelchair to get around. I can walk if I wear full leg braces and use my crutches. If I didn't have anything for support, I couldn't walk because I have feeling in my legs but not my feet. I'll probably have to use a wheelchair the rest of my life. I'm not angry about things, instead I feel blessed with the mobility I have. Also, I'm one of 22 kids chosen by the U.S. Department of Health and Human Services to create a national campaign to prevent bullying in schools. That's cool!

Meredith, 10

I have cerebral palsy, which is a disorder that affects my muscle coordination and movement. I have a wheelchair, but mostly I use my walker. I have to keep being active so I don't get worse. I'm in Girl Scouts, and I took tap dance when I was four. So it's not like I'm sitting at home in front of the television. For exercise, I swim and ride my horse. Riding has improved my balance, and helps make my muscles stronger. Also, I go three days a week to this place where they have exercise tables. I could just lay there and all these machines would do everything for me. But when my mom's there, she makes me work. I call her the "drill sergeant."

Autumn, 11

I'm in the sixth grade and I have ovarian cancer, which is crazy at my age. The doctors told us that ovarian cancer doesn't exist in children. But I have it! I was diagnosed at age five. I had ten surgeries, and all kinds of chemo treatments, but I kept relapsing, which means the cancer came back. Since the chemo treatments weren't curing me, the doctor did a stem cell transplant, which replaces bad, cancerous cells with healthy cells. It was a shot in the dark. The doctor told us that this hadn't been done before with my kind of cancer, but we needed to try it to save my life. I've been okay since the stem cell, but if I have another relapse, there's nothing they can do to save me. I have to get tested every few months to see if the cancer has returned. I can't tell you how scary those tests are, and to know that just one result can change everything.

Ivy, 11

I have a brain tumor, and I'm in a wheelchair. I speak English and Spanish fluently, although I've had a little trouble speaking since my operation. Being paralyzed felt stupid. Just sitting there and not being able to move or to tell your feelings was frustrating, and I got angry. I consider myself courageous. One of my goals is to walk without using a walker or wheelchair. I am determined to go from being totally paralyzed after my brain surgery to totally walking.

José, 11

Call me "Little Bro." I have Ewing's sarcoma, a cancer on the outside of the bone. I've had cancer four times and have come out of remission four times. I've had 16 surgeries. I'm sick of all the surgeries and really hope the cancer doesn't come back again. The doctors don't know if it will. That's kinda scary, when the professionals can't say. I'm a nice kid who cares a lot for people. It's hard being me. I've been through a lot.

Sarah, 11

When I was two, I was diagnosed with leukemia, which is cancer of the blood. I received treatments and went into remission; but I had a relapse when I was eight. I spent a lot of time in the hospital because of my treatments. I actually didn't hate the hospital as much as most people; I even had fun and made some good friends there. I also started a business and made money while I was in there.

Scotty, 11

I have multiple sclerosis (MS), a disease that attacks the nervous system. It's very rare for a kid to get MS. At age nine I thought I was walking fine, but my mom says I wasn't, so we went to the doctor and found out I had MS. Also, I can't see very well in my right eye, and in my left eye my center vision is blocked. The doctors are trying to figure out if there is some connection between the MS and the vision. I was stable for a while, and then I relapsed and lost most of my mobility. I'm in a motorized wheelchair, but just for now, I hope.

Hope, 12

I have osteosarcoma in my knee, which is a cancer growing out of the bone. The tumor started in my knee and spread to other parts of my body, which is why they can't operate on me. I'm totally determined to beat this! When my friends and family get upset, I always tell them, "I'm going to be fine." I was always very athletic—I played basketball and was a cheerleader. I'm being homeschooled now and really miss my friends and going to school. When I learned I had to get chemo, I said, "I don't mind the chemo, as long as I don't lose my hair." I want to be famous, like have my own talk show, which I'll call "Hoprah."

Jessica, 12

I have acute lymphoblastic leukemia, also called t-cell ALL. It's a cancer in my bone marrow, and it's not fun. I was diagnosed a year ago. I'm in remission now. I missed the first couple months of school, but I go to school when I can. When I grow up, I want to work with dogs. I don't know if I want to be a vet, but I love dogs! Before I got cancer, I played soccer, volleyball, and basketball, and ran track. Cancer has slowed me down. It's frustrating, but I was lucky they caught it early. I'm going to play soccer again. I didn't play last year, but instead of getting trophies, my team got sweatshirts with my name and "Soccer Cats" on them.

Justin, 12

I was born with a hole in my heart. Then I got leukemia. I almost died because the doctors misdiagnosed my cancer and thought I had a broken arm. I had open-heart surgery when I was 10. I've also had a bone marrow transplant. I'm in sixth grade. I don't make good grades in school, when I actually make it to school. I LOVE reptiles! I like swimming, bike riding, and air softing, which is like paintball but with tiny plastic pellets.

Mookie, 12

My real name is Haydee, but everyone calls me Mookie. I have diabetes, meaning my body does not produce or properly use insulin, which is needed to convert sugar into energy. I also have Hodgkin's disease, which is a cancer that attacks the body's immune and blood-forming systems. I think I'm funny, outgoing, and the type of person who makes a lot of friends. I play softball and basketball. I don't wear dresses unless someone makes me. I'm homeschooled, but I'm going back to school in January. I'm not going to tell anyone at school about my cancer. They don't need to know. The most important thing I think people should know is that it doesn't matter if I'm sick or not, I'm still gonna always be myself. You are always who you are no matter what.

Nadia, 12

I have FSGS, which stands for focal segmental glomerulosclerosis. The doctors took my kidneys out when I was three because they were actually working *against* my body, hurting me more than helping me. I was on the waiting list for a new kidney for four years until I finally had a kidney transplant. But after a year, they took it out because my body rejected it. I don't have kidneys right now; so I have to do dialysis every night for 10 hours while I sleep. A dialysis machine takes the place of your kidneys to clean your blood. I have a permanent tube coming out of my stomach for dialysis. I'm afraid of kids making fun of me if they see it, so I wear loose-fitting clothes to hide it. I've had 50 surgeries. My doctors say that I'm a walking miracle.

Abbie, 13

I have a cancer called medulloblastoma, which is a tumor in the back of my brain. It could have been there since birth, but we don't have any family history of cancer. In an operation, the doctors got every last trace of it. I try not to worry that the cancer might come back. I think more about normal things, like friends and school. I play sports, and I'm a very outgoing person. I have a lot of friends, and I love animals, art, and writing.

Elyse, 13

I have a severe brain injury because of a car accident when I was 11. A kid ran a stop sign and hit us, and my brother died in the accident. I'm still angry about it because nothing happened to the boy who caused it. Before the accident I was a social butterfly, and I played soccer. Now, I can't play sports, and some of my friends from before don't talk to me. I have paralysis in my left arm, and I have problems walking long distances. I have a wheelchair for *really* long distances. I've made a lot of new friends, and my fashion statement is to wear a bunch of safety pins on my clothes.

Aaron, 15

Just so there's no confusion with the spelling of my name, I'm a girl. I have acute myelogenous leukemia or AML. Leukemia is cancer in your blood, and the kind I have is really aggressive and hard to stop. I was diagnosed with it when I was 12. Before I got cancer, you could never call my phone. It would always be busy because I would talk, talk, talk. Now I don't talk a lot, especially in the hospital. I've had seven surgeries and a ton of chemotherapy, but it's not working. I'm having a bone marrow transplant next week to try to stop the cancer. If it doesn't work, I'm out of options, which means I'll probably die. I don't want to die. There are too many things I want to do in life.

Amber, 15

I have osteosarcoma in my right shoulder; it's a rare bone cancer that kids get. I went through 12 rounds of horrible chemotherapy treatments. They were going to cut out the tumor, but that meant removing my arm, shoulder, and cutting into my chest. They didn't do the operation because it was too dangerous. I still have the tumor, and it has spread to other parts of my body. Sometimes I have difficulty breathing. They can't do anything to save me. They tell me that I'm going to die, and it could be real soon. I know I'm not going to live to see my next birthday, so I got my friends together and we planned this great birthday party for me. I told them to have the same party when I'm gone and not be sad on my birthday.

Brittney, 15

I'm like any other teen, but a little shy. I like to hang out with my friends, go to the beach, shop, and go to the movies. I like to play rock and pop music on my electric guitar. I would describe my medical condition as "crappy." I was first diagnosed with congenital nephritic syndrome, then Denys-Drash syndrome, and then PTLD (post-transplant lymphoproliferative disorder) manifesting as lymphoma in my neck. I've had 75 surgeries, including a kidney transplant when I was one. My brother and I have the same syndrome and have had many different serious illnesses. I can't have any more chemo because I've had so much, and I'm pretty much out of options. If I relapse, there is nothing they can do to save me, so I live every day to the fullest.

Javlyn, 16

I was born with a blood disorder called sickle cell anemia. My parents didn't have the disease, just the traits. You can't die directly from sickle cell, but you can die from complications from the disease. I have had numerous crises and five surgeries. I had my spleen removed at the age of four, and my gallbladder removed at the age of eight. I have a lot of pain and take 15 pills a day. I have spent more than half my life in the hospital. I think I'm pretty strong for dealing with this. I try to handle things the best I can. I don't want to be different. I started a sickle cell support group.

Marian, 16

I have juvenile rheumatoid arthritis, which is a rare condition. I have the systemic type, which is the rarest and most dangerous kind. It affects all my joints, and it can affect my heart, lungs, liver, spleen, and I get chest pains. There are no cures. I'm stuck with it forever. I don't know if it will get worse or not. I'd be a lot different if I didn't have arthritis because I wouldn't have as much sympathy for others. I don't think I'd be as glad to be here and thankful for the good I have in life. I wish people understood arthritis and knew the difficulties I go through. When I tell people I'm sick, they don't believe me because it's not always visible.

Mason, 16

I had osteosarcoma, a bone cancer, just above my right knee. They found it last year. They took out my knee and the bone above and below it, and replaced it with metal and other materials. I have a big scar on my leg and skin grafts from the operation. They got all of the cancer out, and I don't have to have any more chemo. I have to get scans every six weeks to make certain nothing returns. I love to listen to music, sing, and write music. I play bass guitar, drums, trombone, and piano. I also love to travel and learn about different cultures. I played baseball, football, and I ran track. It sucks not being able to run, but I know that I'll play sports again. I never really think of it as a negative. My leg still hurts every once in a while, mostly when I sit too long and then I have to stretch it out.

Charon, 18

I was diagnosed with osteosarcoma cancer two years ago, and I had to have my whole left leg amputated to try and stop the cancer from spreading. The day I found out that I had cancer was the same day my father died of a heart attack. These things changed my life forever. People look at me and think I can't do stuff because I only have one leg, but I try to do everything other people do. I don't ask for help unless I really need it, because I don't want to feel like I'm worthless. I try to do everything I can. I love music and I LOVE football. Cancer changed my life in a positive way—it made me a better person.

Ryan, 18

I was born with cerebral palsy, but I'm not all busted up about it. I'm thankful for my disability being a mild case. It's not something that should be looked down upon. It is what it is. That's why I believe I'm like this—I have a disability and I go through what others go through. But I can talk about it so others can see it's not the end of everything. I've never walked, and it will never happen. I have bad knees, and my hip sockets aren't formed. I don't know what it's like to be able to walk. If you have never walked, you never miss it. People who walked at one time and can't anymore know what they are missing, and they're bitter as hell about it. I am not like that.

Blayne, 19

I have three separate afflictions. I have a mild form of cerebral palsy. I also have spina bifida occulta, which means my spinal cord is exposed to the rest of the inside of my body. In addition, I have tethered cord syndrome, a cord that didn't attach in my spinal cord wrapped around my spine and tightened as I grew. All of these are completely separate things that happened to the same person. When I was born, they thought I only had cerebral palsy. When I was 14, they found the other two. If the tethered cord is found and removed early on, nothing bad happens. But since they found it when I was 14, it did damage that can't be fixed. Even though I have cerebral palsy, it's more the tethered cord syndrome and the spina bifida that you see in the way that I walk. Extensive therapy and medicine has helped me become more mobile.

Miriam, 19

I'm a cancer survivor! I was diagnosed with Hodgkin's disease when I was 14, did the chemo, and then relapsed 17 months after my first diagnosis. I've had five surgeries, a lung biopsy, and a stem cell transplant. I've been cancer-free now for two years. Oh, I'm happier than a tuna! Most people are afraid of cancer, but the only thing I'm afraid of is me. I know what I'm capable of—I just don't know my limits. My motto was, "Cancer is not going to control me. I'm going to control the cancer." I don't really have any hobbies, except talking.

Alan, 20

I have ischemic anoxic brain injury. I tried to commit suicide six times, starting when I was eight. All of my disabilities are due to my last suicide attempt five years ago. I ended up in a wheelchair from lack of oxygen to my brain, and I can't speak. I have a computer that I type into that speaks for me. I'm just starting to talk and use my legs a little. I walked across the stage with a walker for high school graduation, which was a big deal for me. Before my suicide attempt, I was the class clown, and I'm still very playful. People tell me I have a great laugh and an expressive face. I love practical jokes! I'm studying English in college and want to be a writer. I like hanging out with friends, watching movies, and listening to music, with my favorite being alternative rock—the louder the better.

Catyche, 20

I was born with sickle cell anemia, a genetic disorder. I have SS, the worst kind. Sickle cell is extremely painful, so I live on pain medicine. I get sick with pneumonia a lot, and a couple of times, I almost died, and once was in a coma for a week. The doctors even talked with my parents about taking me off of the ventilator that was keeping me alive. I've been in a wheelchair and on oxygen for a year. I get really angry and depressed about my illness. People should know that I'm normal and I'm just like you. My problem is doctors—they never really have a definite answer for my illness. I think I'm very determined. I can be shy when I don't know people, but once I get to know you, I'm very outgoing and gregarious.

Faith, 20

I was born with HIV, but I didn't find out about it until I was 12, when my mom died from AIDS. None of us kids knew about it, just that our mother was sick a lot. We all got tested after she died. I'm the only kid who got HIV, I guess because I was the last born. I don't think that's fair, and it makes me angry. Then my dad got murdered. He was a security guard and got shot. Everyone in my family knows that I'm HIV-positive, but I don't dare tell anyone else. I'm afraid they won't want to be my friend. I don't even go to support groups because I don't want anyone to see me there. I have to take medications for the rest of my life. They said they're working on a cure, but I don't believe it 'cause I don't think they're trying hard enough.

Tonya, 20

I have spina bifida. I had four heart attacks in the first weeks of my life, and I actually died all four times, but the doctors brought me back to life. One time, my heart stopped beating for two and a half minutes and the doctors pronounced me dead. I also was born with a blood vessel pressing on my windpipe causing breathing problems. The doctors removed several of my ribs when I was an infant in order to remove the blood vessel. They said I wouldn't live past a few days, but I proved them wrong! When I was eight, they found that I had fluid on my brain. They put an eight-foot tube in my body from my brain to my stomach. They put in that much length for when I grew, but I never grew, and it's all curled up inside me. I've never been to school. The school people told my mama I wouldn't live long enough to be taught anything; now I can't read or write. I pray every night to be able to walk. It makes me happy to think I could walk.

Jonathan, 21

I have Duchenne muscular dystrophy, a fatal and deteriorating muscular disease. I was diagnosed within a week of my birth. I knew about my muscular dystrophy early on because I stumbled a lot. For the first 10 years of my life, I enjoyed many of the "normal" things kids do. In my teens, my physical strength and agility declined rapidly. I became completely dependent on my wheelchair. In my late teens, I lost mobility in my arms and my parents had to start feeding me. I hated having my parents feed me like I was a baby. I had to have a special wheelchair that could lie back. My heart and lungs began pressing against each other, and my doctors said I would die before my 17th birthday—they were wrong! I completed high school through homeschooling and maintained above-average grades. Most of the time I have a good attitude, but sometimes I get depressed, especially when people stare at me in public.

Luke, 22

I have Hodgkin's disease, a cancer that takes over your lymph nodes. I was diagnosed a month before my 17th birthday. I then developed myelodysplastic syndrome (MDS), which is when defective blood cells take over healthy blood cells, causing lots of diseases. I then developed Evans' syndrome, which is another rare blood disorder. Cancer doesn't run in my family at all. This was kind of a fluke. I'm in and out of the hospital a lot, which means I can't plan long-term things.

Chapter 1
Finding Out

"Cancer has made me aware that anything can happen to anyone at any time. You think you're invincible at 15, and it hits you. Anything can happen to anyone at any time." —Mason

"I'd always tell myself, 'There's always a reason for this to happen. There has to be something good that will come out of this.'" —Abbie

"Cancer has given me a much stronger relationship with God, and it's made me a lot shorter." —Justin

---

Some of us were born with our illnesses and always knew about them. But some of us seemed fine until one day we started having aches and pains, or something didn't seem right, and we went to the doctor. Here we talk about how we found out that life was never going to be the same again.

Safe . . . at First
Mason, 16

During the summer before the tenth grade, I hurt my right knee playing baseball by sliding back into first base. The pain would go away with aspirin, but it always came back. I finally got an MRI (magnetic resonance imaging) done. My mom was in the room with me, and the doctor was pretty shook up when he saw the MRI. He said it was a tumor, and there was a chance it could be cancerous.

When I first heard the word *tumor*, I wasn't exactly sure what it was. I just knew it was bad. I thought, "What? That has to be wrong!" That was the only time I was really upset. We got a biopsy the same day.

> **bi-op-sy:** removal of tissue from the tumor to test it for cancer
>
> **MRI:** a diagnostic procedure that produces detailed images of organs and structures in the body

A few days later, my dad was sitting outside on the porch. I went out to him and he solemnly said the hospital had called. He said, "It's cancer, but it's treatable and we'll get through this." I wasn't upset because somehow I already knew that it would be cancer. I don't know why. I never thought it could kill me. I just said, "What do I have to do to beat this thing?" I never had a negative attitude.

The first time I saw the tumor was during the bone scan of my right knee a few days later. It showed up bright white. I said, "This %$#*! picked the wrong body." I was thinking about Lance Armstrong because he said the same thing.

> **he-mo-phil-ia:** a disorder that prevents blood from clotting properly, making it difficult to control bleeding, even from minor cuts
>
> **port:** an outlet surgically implanted under the skin so the patient can regularly receive medicine without numerous needle sticks

I Always Remember Having Hemophilia
Matthew, 9

At five months of age, I started developing raised bruises on my chest. When my mom would pick me up, I'd get this big bruise wherever her thumb touched me. My parents had me tested, and I had hemophilia.

My first memory of finding out was when I was five years old and got my second port put in.

The first port had gone bad because they last for only so long. The thing I remember most is that they changed the location of my port. My first port was in my chest. When I woke up from surgery, my mom told me that they put the new port in my belly. I didn't believe her and got really angry. I said, "No, they didn't. Stop making that up!" My mom had to actually show me.

Later, my aunt explained my anger to my mom. She said, "Think about it, imagine if someone said to you, 'We're going to take your belly button and put it on your nose.' Your belly button has been in one spot since you've been born; the idea of putting it on your nose just doesn't make sense. He's known his port, since he was a baby, only in his chest."

I grew up knowing that every other day I got a shot. I thought it was what all kids did. When I finally understood I had hemophilia, what that actually meant, and that we could control it, I felt better knowing. It didn't bother me that I had something other kids didn't have. My way of learning about it was my parents involving me in the process of controlling it. At age two, they let me pick out my bandages. At age three, I was unpacking my medical supplies. They did that so I would know what was going on and not be afraid. I never had a big, "Ah-ha!" moment.

I Never Thought "Why Me?"
Luke, 22

As a junior in high school, I had a large lump in my chest; when I exercised I had a hard time breathing. The first doctor I went to said I was just really out of shape, and I must have hit myself in the chest without realizing it. I thought that doctor was an idiot for saying that—I think I'd remember if I got hit that hard in the chest. I waited a couple more months, and then I saw another doctor. That doctor said, "I think you have a tumor." He sent me in **for** a CAT scan that day.

CAT scan: similar to an x-ray, but a more detailed picture inside the body

Hodg-kin's dis-ease: a cancer in the lymphatic system that causes the cells to abnormally reproduce, eventually making the body less able to fight infection

Lymph nodes: tissue that acts like a filter to remove germs that can harm the body

che-mo-ther-a-py/ che-mo: special medicines to treat cancer by trying to kill cancer cells

ra-di-a-tion: high energy rays used to shrink or kill cancer cells

I didn't think it was going to be anything serious. When they told me it was cancer, I didn't know what to think. They explained that it was a cancer of the lymph nodes. They did a biopsy, and took a piece out, but they couldn't take the whole tumor out, so I had to do chemotherapy and radiation. They took a piece of my rib, too, to see if the cancer was in the bone. Luckily, it wasn't. But my lymph node had Hodgkin's.

I never went through the "why me?" stage. It's better me than if it was one of my sisters—it would be really hard for me to see them as sick as I am.

Just a Feeling I Had
Hope, 12

One day in August, me and my best friend, Emily, were riding our new scooters together. We both looked back at the same time and ran into each other. I hit my right knee, which is where my cancer started. I had a hunk of skin torn out of my knee and 12 stitches. It really hurt.

I was getting over the accident and was trying out to be cheerleader. I had to teach myself everything, like tumbling, cartwheels, and jumps. I worked very hard, and I made it. I was a cheerleader! My knee would get sore during cheerleading. My mom would tell me, "Stop jumping, and wait and see what happens."

It never got better. I couldn't stand and put pressure on it. I started limping. We went to the doctor, and he thought I had just sprained my knee. I had this fear in the back of my head that it could be a tumor. I asked my mom, "What if it's a tumor?" She said, "It's probably not going to be." It was just a feeling that I had.

The doctor sent us to an orthopedist (a doctor who specializes in the skeletal structure of the body), who took an x-ray. He said, "I think I see something. I want the oncologist (a doctor who specializes in treating patients with cancer) to look at it." My mom and I just looked at each other. He saw something but wasn't telling us.

Riding in the elevator to see the oncologist, I thought the worst thoughts you could think. They took another x-ray of my knee and thigh. I also had a CAT scan, a bone scan, and an MRI. The bone scan scans every part of your body, the whole skeleton. It's this doughnut thing, and it goes along inches from your body. You have to lay there and be still for three hours! They put an IV in me to help me relax.

They told us that it looked like it could be a tumor. There was definitely something there, and the doctor wanted to do a biopsy. After the biopsy, they put my family in a small, private waiting room. Later the doctor told them the news, that

os-te-o-sar-co-ma: a cancer that affects bones and is generally found in children and teens

I had osteosarcoma cancer, and it had spread to both legs, my hip, two vertebrae, my lungs, and a spot on my shoulder. My parents were absolutely stunned.

My mom's the one who told me I had cancer. I remember her coming in while I was in the recovery room. I asked her, "What's going on? Why am I still here?" I was just coming out of anesthesia, so I was still foggy. When she told me I had cancer, I was in shock. I never realized how serious it could get. I guess it's good that I was groggy. I really cried my eyes out when I found out that I was going to lose my hair. I hated my red hair, until it fell out. Now I really appreciate my hair, even if it is red. At least it's hair. The really weird thing is that you're meeting new people who were strangers 20 minutes ago, and now your life is in their hands.

Sadness Led Me to This
Alan, 20

I tried to commit suicide six times, starting when I was eight. My last attempt left me in my current condition. I was recognized as severely clinically depressed. I was having problems coping with life. I was very angry with my parents. The smallest disappointment from anyone would cause me severe bouts of depression.

After one very bad week, I overdosed with my psychiatric drugs. At the hospital, they pumped my stomach without protecting my airway. I developed ARDS (acute respiratory distress syndrome), and aspirated into my lungs, scarring my lungs. Then I had to have lung surgery, and in the process they placated my diaphragm, which is probably another reason why I have speech problems.

When I regained consciousness, I was on a ventilator because my lungs were so damaged. Then I developed a hole in my right lung. They didn't get it closed fast enough, and I suffered hypoxic brain injury. I had eight more holes in my lungs that had to be patched in the following months. I went into a coma for the next few months. I recovered from that, but couldn't move any part of my body.

ARDS: a life-threatening lung failure when the lungs fill with fluid and collapse

Mine Started with Red Polka Dots

Sarah, 11

When I was two, I had real low energy, and I bruised easy. When I broke out with little red pin dots around my face, my mom took me to the doctor. He did a blood test and he could tell by the results I had cancer, because my white blood cell count was really high and my red blood cell count and platelets were really low. When your platelets are low, your blood vessels under your skin can break—that's what caused the dots.

They put me on chemo for two and a half years when I was two years old. I went into remission (when the signs and symptoms of cancer disappear in response to treatment) when I was five, so I started school with my friends. When I was eight, they gave me a routine bone marrow spinal tap test, which they have to do once you are cured to make sure the cancer hasn't come back.

My mom always got nervous about me having my tests, because she knew that at any time we could get bad news. We always hated every time the phone rang after the tests. Either they don't call, which is good news, or the nurse calls and says, "Everything's fine." The big joke in cancer families is, "If the doctor calls, as soon as you hear his voice, you know something is wrong."

My dad picked up the phone and heard, "This is Dr. Golembe." He knew right then. My dad called for my mom to get on the phone. They were on the phone for so long, us kids knew something BIG was up.

After they got off the phone, my parents were upstairs for a half hour. I found out later they were trying to decide whether to tell me right away or wait. They came down, turned off the television, and told all three of us kids, because it mattered to all of us. My parents wanted us to know everything. I knew that there was a possibility that I could die, but the important thing is my parents never lied to me. They told me we were going to fight it, like we did before.

red blood cells: deliver oxygen to the body tissues and protect the body against infections by attacking and destroying bacteria, virus, or other organisms

white blood cells: often used to find an infection or to see how the body is dealing with cancer treatment

plate-lets: cells in the blood that help the blood to clot when a person is bleeding

I Was Never Sick

Jessica, 12

I was absolutely never sick growing up. NEVER! I might catch something that went around school, but other than that, my mom took me to the doctor only for yearly checkups.

I had a basketball jamboree and did quite well. I went to the doctor the next day because we thought I had a cold. When my parents took me in, I had red, flushed cheeks and little red dots on my torso. The dots would go away and come back, but we didn't worry about them. I did a urine test. It came back full of white cells! The doctor said, "That's not normal. We're going to run some blood work."

I wasn't happy about that, but no one was worried. The nurse and a couple of her colleagues came in, and they were looking at me and poking me. We thought, "Well, this is pretty hands on." After the blood work, she asked for our number to call us the next day with the results. We were still thinking it was no big deal. We went home and two hours later the phone rang.

The doctor said, "She's been admitted to Emanuel Hospital, and you need to get her there now!" We didn't even know where Emanuel was. They wanted to wait until we got to the hospital to tell us the diagnosis because they didn't want my mom driving upset. But my mom made them tell her the news on the phone. I heard my mom say "leukemia." Then she started screaming, "What!"

> **leu-ke-mi-a:** a cancer of the blood

I had no clue what it was. I was really scared. Cancer came up. Cancer is a scary word. You immediately think you're going to die. I felt like I was going to puke. We'd lost my aunt Debbie several years ago to breast cancer.

It goes back to the doctor who diagnosed me. She was a chief resident and went through the cancer program, so she knew what to look for. We were lucky. The previous doctors who we had were totally unconcerned because they didn't know what to look for, and thought it was nothing. When we got to the hospital, it took them forever to get an IV started on my arm. Three days later, I had surgery to have a port put in. Then they did a bone marrow test to find out how far along the cancer was. They told us that they caught it very early. They started chemo that night.

I Thought I Was Going to Die!

Abbie, 13

I was a big basketball player. I played point guard. During our championship game, I was falling all over the place—not playing like I usually do. I didn't score any points. That was one of the first things we noticed.

Then, close to the end of school, I had to use the wall for balance when I walked. I was constantly losing my balance and getting really bad headaches.

We had no idea it was really anything serious. My friends and I would joke about it. They would say, "Oh, you've got cancer!" or, "It's a brain tumor!" Then one Sunday night, I was playing third base in a softball game. Someone hit a line drive at me, and I put my glove out to get it, but it hit my other hand. My dad pulled me out of the game and the next day took me to the doctor.

After a CAT scan, the doctor called us at home and said I had to come back in. I was upstairs getting ready for swim practice when the call came. My mom and brother were downstairs, and my mom was crying. I went downstairs to see what she was crying about. She wouldn't tell me at first. Finally, she said, "Abbie, they found something." I knew it was cancer. I yelled, "I TOLD you so!" I thought there was something wrong with me, but my mother kept saying, "Honey, there's nothing wrong with you."

I flew out the front door screaming. My mom had to tackle me in the front yard. I was crying and screaming, "I told you I had something wrong! Am I going to die?" It was horrible! My mom just held me and said, "It's going to be okay." My brother came up to me outside and I told him, "My life is ruined. I'm going to die." He said, "No, Abbie, no!" He was trying to comfort me, and then he started crying. It was scary.

We went straight to the hospital, and we had friends there waiting for us. That was really neat. That night, I had a lot of friends come and visit. I was mad and angry—at everything. I didn't know what was going to happen to me. Of course, I cried.

At noon the next day, I went into surgery for seven hours to have the tumor removed from my brain. Luckily, they got it all out. The doctor was really cool about my hair. He flipped it up and shaved underneath it, so that when it dropped back down you couldn't see where I had been shaved. Of course, later, it all fell out anyway.

They Kept Insisting Nothing Was Wrong
Charon, 18

I started having persistent knee pain in October of my sophomore year. The doctor kept saying it was just a sprain, and kept sending me home with pain pills.

By July, the pain really started hitting me. Sometimes, I couldn't even walk. I told my friends, "Man, my knee hurts." They jokingly said, "Just wait and see, you're gonna get your leg cut off."

Then one day, my leg was stuck bent and I couldn't straighten it. I went to the hospital, and they still said it was just sprained. We went through a hard time during all this because they kept saying there was nothing wrong. They acted angry because I kept coming back to the hospital—like it was my fault that they couldn't figure anything out. They were so annoyed at me. My mom thinks it was a racial thing because we are black. All they took was one x-ray, and they wouldn't take any more because they didn't see a problem. We never saw the x-rays. The cancer had been growing in my knee up to a year before I even felt it, so it should have been seen in the x-ray.

Then in August, I found out I had cancer. The same day we found out I had cancer, my dad had a massive heart attack and passed away. He was 42 and had high blood pressure. I was lying in my bed when I heard my mom yelling and screaming and carrying on. I got up and my knee was hurting. I walked into their room and my dad was in bed. I thought I was in a dream. He was already gone. He went really quick. All he ever said was, "I don't feel good." He just lay down on the bed, and he was gone.

Two hours later, I was at the doctor's finding out that I had cancer. I wasn't worried about the cancer. I was more upset about my dad. I didn't want to go into the hospital until after the funeral.

A couple of days after my dad's funeral, they took a biopsy. I opted to stay awake, rather than being put under. The nurse put some stuff on my knee to numb it, but it didn't work. The nurse pulled out these big needles and punched them all over my knee. She did seven of them, putting the needle right into where the tumor was and drawing out cells. The pain was unlike anything I'd ever felt. I should have been put under.

They called us a few days later and confirmed that I had cancer. I had to go into the hospital that next week to start treatments. The tumor was right above the knee, which meant I couldn't straighten my knee. I don't remember all of what the doctor said. I just remember him talking about cancer, and they're gonna save my life. I like that he cares about the kids, and he's honest. He tells us everything up front. He went on a little bit about losing my hair. I told him, "As long as you save my leg, I don't care."

My mom thinks that if they had caught it sooner, I might not have lost my leg. I have no idea. Everyone's cancer grows differently, so I can't say I would still have my leg. I might have more of my leg, but I probably would have lost some of it.

We Really Needed Some Humor
Brittney, 15

My parents didn't know I was sick until I was about a year old. I started projectile vomiting, and my mother took me to the doctor. They kept saying it was pneumonia, but I didn't have those symptoms. I gained a pound and a half of water weight in less than 24 hours. My mother kept taking me back; and they finally sent us to the children's hospital. There, on my first birthday, I was diagnosed with congenital nephritic syndrome. When we got to the children's hospital, I was in total kidney failure.

I had multiple surgeries, including removal of my kidney three months later. I was placed on dialysis. I later learned I had Denys-Drash syndrome and the congenital nephritic syndrome was underlying. They told my parents that, since they thought I only had congenital nephritic syndrome, my parents should be able to have more children and they would be fine. My brother, Jordan, was born four years later with the same disease. Actually, it's rare that we both have it. That sucks. There is not really much known about Denys-Drash, which also sucks.

> **ne-phrit-ic syn-drome:** an inflamation of the kidneys, causing them to leak protein from the blood into the urine
>
> **Denys-Drash syn-drome:** a disorder with three main parts: kidney disease, kidney cancer, and malformation of the reproductive organs
>
> **di-al-y-sis:** process where a machine takes the place of the kidneys to remove waste from the blood

My mother was the donor for my kidney. My father was the donor for my brother. I was 22 months old when I had my kidney transplant. When doctors put an adult kidney into a baby, they take it out of the donor, rinse it, and squish it down as much as they can without damaging it. Then they put it in front of my belly, under the skin. We have home videos and it looks like I'm pregnant—I even waddle. Eventually, it shrinks down to the size that I need and adapts to my body.

For my mom, they just took out her kidney, gave her some pain meds, and she went home and was fine. For me, things changed big time. To keep my body from rejecting the kidney, I was on immune suppressive drugs, which kill your immune system and make you susceptible to all childhood illnesses. I was having horrendous fevers, and I slept a lot and stopped eating.

Im-mune sys-tem: the body's natural protection from disease

I went into the hospital on September 11. Yeah, that September 11. They were running tests to figure out what was wrong with me while my mom and I watched the Twin Towers getting blown up. We were crying. We hurt for those people.

Then the doctors came in and said, "Oh, you have cancer." They had done a chest x-ray and found a tumor in my lung. They immediately started doing CAT scans and all these other tests, and found that I had these cyst things in my lungs, liver, and lymph nodes. I was basically in the third stage, meaning that some of the cancer may be removed in an operation, but some of it cannot be removed and remains in the abdomen or in the lymph nodes. There were 12 tumors in my liver alone. The one in my lung was the size of a golf ball and was tangled in layers of nerves. They had to do an open-lung biopsy on me.

I wasn't scared because I was used to having so many illnesses. My mom thought everything was so tense and so serious that we needed something fun. So my mom wrote a joke on my stomach. Just before I went under, I gave the doctor the punch line. I said, "Fast food." They're like, "Are you hungry?" I said, "No, fast food." They're like, "Do you want a cheeseburger?" I'm like, "No, fast food." Then I went to sleep.

The surgeon saw the joke and stopped everything and had everybody come over and read what my mother wrote on my stomach. It said, "What do you get when you cross a cheetah and a hamburger?" It stopped the surgeon cold. It was really funny. We needed to lighten things up.

When they got in there, they actually had to cut away part of my lung. Then when he went into the lung, the surgeon found that the tumor was encased and it took him seven hours to get the tumor out. They told us it was post-transplant lymphoproliferative disorder (PTLD) lymphoma—a cancer.

PTLD: a cancer that may occur following an organ transplant

Just a Pain . . .
Kimberlie, 10

Just after my ninth birthday, I wasn't feeling well. I wasn't eating, I would pass out, and I'd get big nosebleeds for no apparent reason. I also was very tired and I had a pain in my leg that would not go away. My mom took me to the doctor three times in three weeks, not thinking it was something serious. My mother thought it might be mono because I'm so athletic. I never complain a lot, so when I said, "Oh, my leg hurts," they knew something was up.

On the third visit, I had blood taken. When the doctor asked to speak to my mom alone, I got very worried. When I saw her crying, I knew it wasn't good. I was very scared because I didn't know what it really was. That's when I found out that I had leukemia.

The night that I was diagnosed changed many things for me. All of sudden, I could not go to school or be with my friends, which made me really sad. Some kids dream of not having to go to school and to be able to stay home and watch TV all day. I dream of being in school.

Finding Out I Had More Than Cerebral Palsy
Blayne, 19

I always knew I had cerebral palsy. Due to the religious beliefs of my family, I did not have my first surgery until I was 14. After the surgery, quite by surprise, I found out that I had tethered cord syndrome and it was freezing my spine. I went, "Wait, hold on. My entire life all I heard was, 'You have cerebral palsy.'" I go to this doctor I've never seen before, and he tells me that I have tethered cord syndrome, and that all the other doctors were wrong, and that we have to get this out now.

I was like, "Holy cow! Wait, you have to give me some time. I have school. I have a life." He said, "No, you have to get this out now! We

cer-e-bral pal-sy: a condition that affects communication between the brain and muscles, causing lack of muscle control

teth-ered cord syn-drome: a cord that doesn't attach in the spinal cord, but instead wraps around the spine and tightens as a child grows, preventing free movement

usually take this out in infancy. Now, let's move!" I didn't even know what to think. We scheduled the surgery for the next day.

From the time I was very young, my parents weren't really involved in my medical care. I came to my doctors' appointments alone. I had to go home and tell my mother, "Are you free tomorrow? I've got surgery scheduled. They've misdiagnosed me and everything's wrong, and my whole life is changed." I came home with pages and pages of information from the doctor.

The doctor had said, "Before you talk to your mom, call me and we'll talk to her together." So we called him on the phone, and he explained the whole situation to my mom. Being very unemotional and strong, she took it in and just said, "Well, okay." I know it shook her world. I know it did. She just doesn't show feelings.

You Have the Wrong Room

Aaron, 15

All I had was a sore throat and I went to my pediatrician. She gave me medicine. The medicine didn't work, so she sent me for blood tests to see if it was strep throat. I don't really get sick often. I take so many vitamins and stuff, a sore throat was odd to me.

They did tests and found out that I had leukemia. Up until then, there was never any indication of anything. I didn't know what leukemia was. Everybody was saying "AML" and "leukemia." I'm thinking, "Give me a pill and I'll get better." Finally, somebody said "cancer." I don't remember who it was because when you get diagnosed, a lot of people are in your room—social workers, Child Life specialists, nurses, doctors—it really was crowded. You get confused, but someone said, "How are you coping with the cancer?" I said, "You have the wrong room. I don't have cancer. I have leukemia." She said, "That's cancer." That's how I found out.

I started thinking I was going to die. I was upset, but I believe that everything happens for a reason. I'm really not scared of dying. I'm not really expecting to die, but if I die, I had a good life. I know God has plans for everybody.

My mom found out before me. She was so torn up about it that she was hard to talk to. In the hospital, she kept saying she had to go to the bathroom or kitchen. She'd come back with red eyes. I had to comfort my mom. I still do. I told her that I loved her a lot and that everything happens for a reason, and not to be worried.

I'm told I'm brave. I didn't choose to be brave. I've been given cancer, and to survive this is what I have to do.

Just a Pain in My Ribs
José, 11

I was five, I weighed too much for my age, and I had a pain in my rib that wouldn't go away. My mom was feeling around my rib area and felt a lump. She took me to the doctor who saw the lump and said, "Everything's fine." A week later, we went to the emergency room because I was having trouble breathing. They took x-rays and extracted fluids with a needle from my lump. Then they told us I had Ewing's sarcoma, a cancer.

> **Ew-ing's sar-co-ma:** a cancer on the outside of a bone
>
> **sar-co-ma:** a malignant tumor

I had chemotherapy for six months, and they removed the tumor and one of my ribs. Two years later I had a killer pain in my face. The cancer had come back. It actually would come back three times total in my face. The third time it came back, I lost my vision temporarily. I can't have surgery to remove the tumor in my face because of where it's located between my eyes and my brain.

I can actually feel the cancer before the doctors say it's back. I also know for sure that it's back when I see my mother crying. The doctor always tells my mom first, and my mom tells me. So the pain, then my mother crying—and it's back.

My Battle Scars
Miriam, 19

I was a typical 14-year-old. I worried more about my vanity than anything. One day in my biology class, I felt a lump in my neck. When I got home, I had my mom feel it. Of course, she freaked out. By supper time, I was at Jersey City Medical Center. By ten o'clock, I knew what I had. They said, "It's either cancer or a lung infection." I had had a lung infection before, and I knew it wasn't that. I knew I didn't have bronchitis because I wasn't coughing. I was like, "I have cancer." Right off the bat, I knew it was cancer.

When the doctor told me for sure that it was cancer, me, two cousins, my mom, and my dad were in the oncology department of the hospital. Neither of my parents speak English, just Spanish. Being my own person, I would not have told them anything. So my cousins told them. My mom said, "Oh, maybe it's a bronchial infection." She was in total denial. But I knew what it was, so I was like, "Okay, whatever. I'm sick. I need help."

I had to take life by the horns. I had to be strong for my parents. I had to be strong for my brother. I had to be strong for myself. I was always a "gung ho" kid. Nothing bothered me. I think that's my problem now—nothing ever bothers me. I didn't think I was going to die. I didn't think anything of it. It's just a little problem, but I have to keep on going.

I got bloated from steroids and lost all my hair from chemo. I wasn't embarrassed to have people see me like that. They were my battle scars. Then I had my relapse. My mother knew before I did. She told me in church. My mom goes, "You're going into operation tomorrow." I was mad at her for not telling me sooner. It's my body. I want to know what's going on. I was mad at everyone in my family—they all knew before I did. I felt betrayed.

I Have Cancer, Not a Broken Arm?
Justin, 12

I was two when I was first diagnosed. I was crying all the time, and my arm seemed really tender to the touch. The tenderness just kept getting worse.

When I first went in, the doctors misdiagnosed my cancer as a broken arm, and they put a cast on my arm. They did an x-ray; they couldn't find anything, but they put a cast on it anyway. I was really tiny and maybe they thought the break was so small that it didn't show up on the x-ray.

A few days later, they found out that it wasn't that. By looking at my blood, the white cell count, platelets, and the red cells were all off. They said, "Well, let's send you to an oncologist, just in case." The oncologist said, "I don't really think he has leukemia, but if you feel more comfortable ruling it out, we can go ahead and do the tests." My parents said, "Let's do it and get it over with." They found out that I did have leukemia. Your world comes crashing down.

We did lots of chemotherapy. When I was five, they stopped the treatment and I went into remission. Then I relapsed two and a half years later. I was bruising a lot, I was always in pain, and I was sleeping a lot. Then I had a skateboard accident and cut my head open. It wouldn't stop bleeding for a long time. My parents took me in and had blood tests done.

We went in and everyone was saying, "Oh, it's probably just a virus." I really didn't think that my cancer might have come back. I just thought it was another day in the hospital. Even after I was told that I had cancer again, it took quite a while for it to really sink in. I said, "Oh, no, not again!" We actually raced to the beach on the Oregon coast to have a fun time over Memorial weekend. We needed to have some fun before it all started again.

A Headache to a Coma in Minutes

Ivy, 11

One day when I was nine, I got a headache before school. By the time my mom called the paramedics, I was already in a coma! That was when they diagnosed that I had a tumor in the back of my brain.

A few months earlier, I complained about light headaches. The doctor said I was reading and using the computer too much. So we cut down on computer time and books. After that, I was still having headaches. They never ordered any CAT scans or anything.

When I first arrived at the hospital in a coma, they had to drain fluid from my head because the tumor was bleeding internally. They told us that they were going to do surgery in two days. Five minutes later, they came back and said they had to do it now because I went into a deeper coma. They did the surgery that same day. After surgery, I was in a coma for two weeks, then I was half in a coma and half normal for a week, then completely out of the coma.

The day I woke up, I was totally paralyzed. I had a feeding tube. It took me a month to start talking again. The first thing I said was, "I don't like the feeding tube." They were going to do a test to see if I was able to eat on my own. They said that it was going to be really hard to pass the test because they gave me a really dry cheese sandwich. I ate half of it and they were all amazed. Before we left, I asked, "Can I have the other half?" I was hungry!

Horrible Rashes and Fevers

Marian, 16

I wasn't born with juvenile rheumatoid arthritis. I got it in the summer between fourth and fifth grades. During the summers I went to camp, and I had used tons of sprays and creams for my rash because I was so itchy. I'd wake up at night crying with a fever.

Also, I'd be lying in a chair and suddenly become really stiff. I was having problems walking. I couldn't brush my hair. I couldn't brush my teeth. I got really high fevers, like 105. I'd have tons of blankets on me and I'd be taking them off, and I'd get only a few hours of sleep. Other times, I'd be exhausted and sleep for hours, which is totally not normal for me.

rheu-ma-toid ar-thri-tis: a chronic disease with pain, stiffness, swelling, and sometimes destruction of joints

Then I had a rash all over my entire body. It was bright red and itching. I couldn't sleep at night. I was in such discomfort. I had ice bags to help the itching. My whole body was so itchy that ice was the only thing that helped. I also took oatmeal baths. All my joints hurt, and my fingers would get big and swollen.

I went to tons of doctors, who all had different ideas and treatments in mind, because systemic arthritis has so many different traits. They misdiagnosed me tons of times. At first, the doctors thought I had jammed my fingers. Then they said it was an infection causing the rash. I was like, "I know it's not that." One doctor wanted to do a low-dose of chemo. I was really upset. I was like, "Daddy, I don't want to do that," and I ended up not doing it.

I probably took medications that I shouldn't have been taking due to the misdiagnoses. I was on weird stuff. I was getting steroid shots and taking antibiotics. They gave me prescription allergy pills because they thought I had an allergy. I went to tons of dermatologists (skin specialists), and they couldn't tell me what this rash was. Then I started developing eczema (dry, itchy skin) on top of the rash.

I was really scared. I kept thinking, "Why is this happening to me?" I had been perfectly fine up until fifth grade. I was on track, and I played soccer and basketball. I was doing everything really well—then suddenly I couldn't do anything.

I was finally admitted to the children's hospital. At first, they thought I had leukemia because the symptoms were like leukemia. They actually diagnosed it by my rash because it's a really unique rash. The rash looks like somebody splattered paint on me. Sometimes it's speckled and sometimes it's a huge spot. When it was really bad, I could draw a smiley face on my leg with my fingernail, and in 20 minutes it would appear. That's what the doctor did to diagnose me. He took a pen with the cap on and drew lines across my back; 10 minutes later the lines were red because of the rash.

I stayed in the hospital for two days, and lost 12 pounds. I see pictures of me then; I looked so bad. I was so tiny and skinny. I was really sick. Also, I was really upset because, when I was first diagnosed, they gave me this book that showed pictures of how you could look with arthritis. My parents got really upset with it because it showed all these kids in wheelchairs. I was like, "I don't want to end up like that."

I Don't Understand—Why Me?

Amber, 15

My right shoulder had been hurting to where I couldn't raise my arm. I played third base in softball, and you gotta have that arm to throw from third base. We just figured it was over-exertion or a pulled muscle. We took a trip to the beach, and I was walking along the beach with my friends and fell over a piece of wood. It was buried in the sand, and I didn't see it. I fell right on my shoulder, and it hurt with more pain than I ever felt. I was crying, and I never cry! It was this sharp pain all the way up the side of my neck and down my shoulder. None of my friends would touch me because they were scared it was something really serious.

We went to the emergency room. I was nervous because I didn't know what was wrong. I thought that maybe it was just a broken shoulder. The doctor came and asked to speak with my mom and dad alone. He told them that it was a tumor the size of a golf ball. He said my shoulder actually broke because of the tumor, not from falling. When my parents told me, I didn't know what to think. I was like, "What's a tumor?" We came home and my mom and dad sat down and discussed it with me. They said it could be cancer. I thought, "If it has to be cancer, why does it have to be me?" Then I thought I need to be positive and kept saying, "It's not going to be cancer; it's not going to be cancer."

They sent us to a specialist to rule out the possibility of cancer. They did two biopsies in the doctor's office, then scheduled an open biopsy because they couldn't get deep enough to get what they needed. I was scared when they did the open biopsy. These awful thoughts were going through my head like, "What if I don't ever wake up? What if I do wake up in the middle of it?" I was so scared.

After we got the biopsy results, they were 100 percent sure it was cancer—osteosarcoma. I was pretty far along. I cried and cried for two days. I didn't know what to think, just, "Why me? Am I gonna die?" Then I said, "I'll get through it one way or another."

The Car Accident

Elyse, 13

I was 11 and my brother was 13. My mom was driving us to school. I was quizzing my brother on the Declaration of Independence. Then the crash happened. A 16-year-old kid ran a stop sign and smashed into our car. My brother died. I was in a coma for two and a half months.

We live in a small community; we don't know personally the kid who crashed into our car, but we know people who know him. He didn't die. I wanted him to go to jail. They said you don't go to jail if you "just run a stop sign." But he killed my brother. He only got charged with running a stop sign. I never talked to the kid who hit us; he never called or anything.

When I was in the coma, from the very get-go they were telling my mother about my condition: "We have no idea. You never know with children. If it was a 35-year-old man, we could give you some ideas. But with kids, they all do better than you would ever guess, so we just can't say."

I don't remember being in a coma, and I don't remember waking up from the coma. The first thing I remember is that a male nurse was changing the sheets on my hospital bed—with me in the bed! I didn't like waking up to that. I pretended like I was still asleep. When he left I said to my mom, "No more male nurses!" They don't usually use male nurses while girls are awake, but they didn't know that I would be awake by that shift.

Chapter 2

Friends and Telling Friends

"Don't treat us any different, but be aware that we are different. **Instead of analyzing those differences, celebrate them.**" —Blayne

"**True friends** are the ones who, when your hair falls out, **help you salvage what's left.**" —Miriam

"Having your friends reject you because you're suddenly 'different' teaches you **how to be a better friend.**" —Elyse

Sometimes the hardest part is telling your friends. It can be for the best, because then they understand why we miss so much school or why we can't spend the night. But sometimes friends never treat you the same again—they don't want to be around us anymore, there are no more party invitations, and that's pretty sad. So we want to tell you about how we told our friends, our advice on telling them, and what you can learn from our experiences.

No One Believed Me
Luke, 22

I didn't tell any of my friends at first. I didn't want to be treated differently. I just wanted things to be normal.

When I told my friends, I told them jokingly. In the middle of a sentence I'd say, "Oh, by the way, I have cancer and I'll be sick," and then resume the sentence. They thought I was just messing with them, because I do that on occasion. It's hard to get people to believe you after you're known for joking around. I guess my delivery didn't help convince them either. They didn't ask a lot of questions. They said, "That sucks!" and "I'm sorry." Some of them asked me if I was going to die. Of course I said, "No! Don't be silly! I just have to take some medicine for a while."

I'm the only one of my friends with a health issue. My friends don't treat me differently. Maybe they were a little nicer to me at first. But now they treat me like anybody else. It's just something that's part of me. I never lost any friends from being sick.

I Love My Friends
Kimberlie, 10

I am very lucky because all my friends have been so great through all of this. They have supported me, uplifted me, and visited me in the hospital. Some of them have even come to my doctor appointments with me. It has meant so much to me that my friends have been so nice, and that our relationships have changed for the better.

You'll See Who Your True Friends Are
Charon, 18

When you find out you have cancer, and you start telling people, you'll see who really cares about you, and who doesn't. When people found out about my cancer, I was surprised at some of the people who I thought were my friends.

The First Person I Told

Amber, 15

The first person I told was my best friend, Megan. I've known her since the second grade. It was real hard. I called her on the phone and said, "I have some bad news. I may have cancer." We cried on the phone for an hour. Then we thought to the positive side and said, "No, it's not going to be." She said, "I'll be here for you no matter what time of night it is. I don't care, call me if you need anything." I thought, now that's a true friend. She said, "We're going to get through it, no matter what." We talked about my cancer, and then we talked about softball. She's on my softball team. Then she said, "Amber, there's something I want to do." I was like, "Megan, you really don't have to do anything but be there for me." She said, "No, I want to do something."

She called me a couple of days later and said, "Amber, I'm going to do a car wash for you." She organized the whole car wash. This was a couple of weeks after I was diagnosed. She said, "I want to get some of our classmates to help." Kids have more energy than the older people. I wasn't feeling good, but I went out there for a couple of hours. It wore me down the next day. I knew I wouldn't be able to stay out there too long because the sun would get too hot on me. They raised $1,400 in four hours! That was so cool. They had a bake sale with it, too.

The hardest part was telling Megan that I was going to die. We cried and cried and cried. There have been times I've been depressed and I'd call people and say, "I've got to talk to somebody just to get my mind off things." I like to talk to people who are older, like Mama's and Daddy's age. There are times I just have to talk to other people. My parents understand that and want me to make memories with friends that I can cherish when times get hard.

Don't Say "I'm Sorry"

Javlyn, 16

When I tell people I have sickle cell most say, "I'm sorry." I say, "Why are you sorry when it's not your fault?" I think they say it because it's the first thing that comes to their mind. Most people don't mean anything by it—it's just a reaction. I wish I was older and was with more mature people because they understand more than kids. When I told my best friend, she sort of understood, but not really. Then, after she saw a program on TV, she understood it more. That's why I want to start the support group—to help those who have it, and to help those who don't understand it.

They Couldn't Handle It
Brittney, 15

To not freak out my friends, my mom would explain things to their parents, and then they would explain it to their kids. The kids wouldn't always get it. Some parents get freaked out when they hear of a kid having cancer. Some of the moms called my mom and said, "Oh, my gosh, I don't want my kid to get close to your kid because what if your daughter doesn't make it?" Stupid stuff like that. People are really ignorant because they don't learn about it. A lot of the friends who we thought were my friends and the parents who we thought were supportive were not.

I told my friends everything so they could get to know me. I'd start naming stuff that I went through. Their jaws would drop. I'd tell them specific things because I didn't want them to be like, "Oh, you've got a disease. Gross!" I would tell my friends I had 48 surgeries. I'd lift up my shirt and show them the scars on my body and they'd ask, "Oh, what's this one for?" I'd make up funny and weird stuff just to have fun with the situation. Some friends asked, if I went bald, if they could they put a huge tattoo on my head. Some of them also said they'd shave their heads for me. Some of my friends were like, "If you need a bone marrow transplant, I'll be a donor."

It's Not All About Lying in Bed
Hope, 12

One of my really good friends wouldn't invite me to her birthday party because she thought I was too sick. It made me really mad. I don't understand why some friends don't get that I'm fine.

I went to get my pictures taken for cheerleading squad. My friends were shocked to see me. I had to go, "Hi," before they burst open and hugged me. Just coming out for the pictures inspired these girls. I said, "I'm still part of this team." It gave them a whole new perspective of what cancer patients are all about. It's not all lying in bed and suffering. Yeah, there is some of that, but then you feel good and you want to be treated normal. Before I had cancer, I thought what my friends think—if you have cancer, you can't do anything. But now I know better.

Explaining Can Turn into a Big Circle
Matthew, 9

My friends don't know I have hemophilia. It's not like I bring it up. If they ask me, maybe I tell them some stuff. I have one friend who knows a little bit. She asked me about my medical bracelet. She has asthma, so she's familiar with certain things. To her it was no big deal. But a lot of kids just don't know enough to understand, even after I explain it. Stuff like infusion, blood clotting factor, and protein are just not part of most kids' daily words, so it's hard for them to really grasp things. It's like two different languages. I'll say, "I have hemophilia." They ask, "What's hemophilia?" I'll say, "It means I'm missing a protein in my blood." They ask, "What's a protein?" I explain and they ask more questions, and it just goes on and on in a big circle.

Sometimes You Can't Tell the Truth
Autumn, 11

If somebody just found out that they have cancer and they have to tell their friends, I would tell them to just be confident in themselves. It was actually pretty easy for me, but I don't know if it would be easy for other people because some people are too scared to express it.

My friends asked me if I was okay, or if I was gonna die. I told them that I was okay, but I didn't know if I was going to die or not, but I believed that I wasn't. They were afraid for me, but they saw how high my spirit was and how I was motivated to do things, so they included me in most things they did. Some friends worried about me, so they didn't want me to do certain things. Sometimes I would even say I was okay even if I wasn't, so they would quit worrying.

My friends think that my life is better because of the things I get, like toys and trips and stuff. I try telling them that my life is not better than theirs, and sometimes we get into arguments. I tell them, "You don't understand what comes with cancer. You can have it, but you ain't gonna want what you get with it."

Friends Were Surprised, But Supportive
Mason, 16

The first person I told was my girlfriend. She didn't really understand it and didn't think that I could have cancer. I told her, "Look, I understand if you don't really want to go through this with me. I won't have any hard feelings against you." She wanted to stay with me, which was cool. Then I called my friend Scott in Washington, D.C., and told him I had cancer. I didn't exactly come out and say it at first. He didn't believe it. He wasn't exactly sure what I meant. We joked around about it. He said that he was going to be a doctor one day, and that he knew everything was going to be all right 'cause he had, like, a doctor's instinct.

Nothing Changed with Some Friends
Charon, 18

I try to make friends with everybody I meet. It's always good to have friends. The cancer and the amputation haven't really changed my friendships. If anyone sees me differently, they don't show it to me. They treat me how I was when I had both my legs walking around school.

When you find out you have cancer, and you start telling people, you'll see who really cares about you, and who doesn't. When people found out about my cancer, I was surprised at some of the people who I thought were my friends.

I told my best friend Jamal that I had cancer. He's the only friend I told, and he was like, "For real? Man, that's messed up. Man, you're gonna get through it." He said positive things.

Then Amy from Child Life came to my school and explained it all to everybody. Child Life specialists are hospital staff who help us in the hospital, and also can go to our schools and explain our illnesses to our classmates. It was the students' choice to go in the gym and hear about what happened to me. She said she walked in there and the whole school was there. It was really cool to hear that! I think Jamal had already told a lot of people about what happened—about my daddy dying suddenly and about my cancer.

After that, though, not too many people called me. Some of the kids wrote letters, but that was only a one-time thing. My good friend Deirdre kind of helped me get through the rest of my treatments after my amputation. She came by and one of her friends came with her, Shamika, and gave me Christmas gifts. I loved it! It put a smile on my face. She still comes by every once in a while, and still calls me.

No Good Response
Aaron, 15

Telling your friends can be very difficult. It's weird 'cause there really isn't a proper reaction from them. Sometimes it makes you feel better if you see someone cry, but at the same time, you don't want to see them upset. If they cry, I know how much they love me and how much I mean to them. But at the same time, I know they're in pain. So there's really no good response to it.

The first person I told was my best friend Marlo. She knew something was wrong because this was my first time ever to go to a hospital. I told her about the cancer, and she got very upset. As I was trying to comfort her, she collapsed and fell on the floor. To this day, I think Marlo is afraid of knowing too much about it because that would make it too real.

I think my friends stopped talking about normal things, because when you get cancer, people don't understand that you're still a person and everything is still going on. Cancer isn't my life, and I do everything in my power to not make it my life. Sometimes it was hard when my friends wouldn't tell me the normal stuff because they thought I wouldn't think it was important any more. The normal details that go on with everyday life are even more important than before. It gets my mind off my cancer and makes me feel normal.

I lost a lot of friends—or people who I thought were my friends. There was this one girl who was my friend for six years. We did everything together. When she found out, she became a different person. She never called me and never came to see me. To this day, I don't dislike her and I don't wish her any bad luck. I just don't think about her at all.

Not Everyone Needs to Know
Lindsey, 10

I told my one really good friend about my situation, and she understands it. I really don't think you need to tell people, unless it matters that they know. I chose to tell my best friend because I wanted her to understand why I have to do some of the things that I do. Sometimes I have to leave in the middle of class, and she was wondering why, so I told her. She hasn't told anybody. Other kids might make fun of me. It's a private issue.

My Friends Were Cool

José, 11

After I found out that the cancer was back, I told my best friend first. He got real quiet. He didn't ask questions or anything. He was a little upset. He knew that I had cancer before. I only told my close friends. None of them treated me differently. They actually took better care of me. It's not like we played rough before, they just kind of took better care of me. None of them really asked any questions.

Most of My Friends Were Cool

Abbie, 13

I told my best friend Morgan, and she told most of my other friends. She didn't really say anything. I couldn't really talk when I told her because I was crying so much, so I just handed the phone to my mom. All of my friends came up that night after my surgery. They were all afraid for me. I think they were trying to be very strong for me, but they were very scared. I just don't think they understood. They asked what was going to happen. We told them that I had a long road ahead of me, but I was going to be fine.

At first, my friends treated me differently, but now they treat me the same. They always made fun of me, and they make fun of me now. When they found out, most of my friends were just nicer to me and gentler around me. It was nice of them, but I actually just wanted to be treated normal. Sometimes I want special treatment, but from adults, not my friends.

Grandma's Disease

Marian, 16

When I explain to people that I have arthritis, I usually tell them the symptoms, and what's wrong with me. Maybe I'll show them a joint that's hurting right then, if it's swollen or something. It's almost incomprehensible because it's not something that most people know about. It's a really rare disease that nobody has. I told my close friends, and I think they understood. If I say, "arthritis," it kinda clicks and they're like, "Oh, my grandma has that." It's like I'm permanently tied to that. I volunteered at the Arthritis Foundation, and some of my friends came and worked with me there.

I think my friends understood better because we were helping kids who had arthritis, and they were complaining of pain.

I'm Afraid to Tell
Nadia, 12

I don't want any of my friends to know about my tube or dialysis, so I don't let anyone spend the night, and I don't spend the night at anyone's house. I'm afraid to tell because I think that if I tell people, they might not want to be my friends. They might think I am weird or something. They would treat me differently because I would have to do dialysis. Doing this book is the first time I've talked about it. My mom can't believe that I'm even talking about this.

Only one of my friends knows. I thought she would freak out, but she didn't. I told her because she's my best friend. I wanted her to spend the night with me. I was nervous about telling her before she had to see my machine. At first, she asked me why I couldn't eat cheese and stuff, and I told her because I have to use dialysis. She asked, "What is that?" I told her that it's something that I have to do that cleans out my body, and I have a machine that I get on every night that helps me do that. She told me that when I get a kidney transplant she's going to have me over to her house to spend the night and go to Taco Bell and get me anything I want!

Some Kids Are Cool
Justin, 12

My friends found out about my cancer from my mom telling their parents. Eventually, they asked me about it. I said, "Yeah, that's happening to me." They were sad for me that I had to go through all of this, but they really didn't treat me any differently. They would bring me pictures and lots of cards and letters to encourage me. They were very supportive. Because of all the radiation and stuff, I'm shorter than kids my age. I've had a few people call me "midget." I don't really care. I have this one really good friend and he's always backing me up, maybe a little too much. He overly defends me instead of keeping cool about it.

I'm Not Telling
Faith, 20

None of my friends know that I'm HIV positive. I think they would treat me differently if they knew. Outside of my family, the only one who knows is my big sister from the Big Sister Program. I don't think I'll ever tell anyone. I don't have many friends anyway, and some of the friends who I've hung around with have already treated me badly. I think that having HIV has made me shy. I still talk to people, but not as much as before. I might tell people when the public gets more educated. When I get married, I'll tell my husband. Other than that, I'm gonna keep it a secret forever. I just want people to know me as a nice person.

Pretty Advice
Miriam, 19

I want to say something to boyfriends and girlfriends of people who are sick. I had a boyfriend when I was sick. It was a test for him. It proved to me that he loved me. He stood by me with all my changes. I felt ugly, and he made me feel pretty, like really pretty. If a person can make you feel pretty in that awkward time, there's nothing more I can say to that.

Prom Date
Amber, 15

I've lost a couple of friends because of my cancer. When they found out I had cancer, they acted ashamed to be around me. The rest have been so sweet. They've treated me really well. Friends come over and we watch movies, and laugh, and cut up about boys. They treat me better than before I got cancer. They don't bring up the cancer, unless I want to talk about it.

It wouldn't bother me any to tell everybody about my cancer. People who I didn't think were my friends became friends after they found out. They'd just pick up the phone and call me. It takes a lot of courage to pick up the phone and call someone that maybe you don't know so well, and ask how they are doing. You cry with them. We sit there and laugh about things, and we talk about boys. It makes a huge difference.

The other day, one of my best friends called and said, "Amber, we want to have a party at my house for you. You invite whoever." I invited a couple of close friends. I thought that was so nice of them to have a party for me.

Not too long ago, my friend Felicia called. She said she'd been thinking about me. She started crying. I said, "I know this may sound awful, but there's going to be one day when you don't have to worry about me suffering or anything because I'm going to be in heaven." Felicia said, "Amber, I don't want to go to the prom with a guy, I want *you* to go to the prom with me." I started crying because most of the time you can't find someone that would do that.

I say to my friends, "Thanks a lot for being there." A lot of people wouldn't think it's important for friends to be there by your side 100 percent of the time, but to me it is. My friends come up and see me at the hospital. They take time out of their weekend, when they could be with their boyfriends and girlfriends, and spend the day with me. It makes me feel real good and means a lot to me.

Chapter 3

Life—the Good, the Bad, and the Downright Ugly

"I try to feel as good as I can today. I don't make plans anymore. I go day by day. But I do live life to the fullest when I feel good because I never know what's going to happen tomorrow." —Luke

"I've had 50 surgeries. My stomach is like a big road map from the scars." —Nadia

"I'd like a morphing wheelchair where it attaches to your legs. **That would be cool."** —Scotty

Everyone has daily hassles, right? We fall down, skin our knees, break things, get stitches—all the stuff that other kids do. But when it happens to us, it's always a little different. Here are the medical realities of our lives—the daily pills, needles, breathing treatments, nightly dialysis, losing hair from chemo, and the other not-so-fun things we have to put up with. It's not really so bad, once you get used to it. And you never have a bad hair day! Despite everything, life is good.

Everything Hurts
Kimberlie, 10

It is hard to explain to people what you have to go through. You worry a lot about fevers, getting sick from other people because your immune system isn't like it used to be, and getting poked with needles. You also have to take medicine that makes you really, really sick. You throw up a lot and your body hurts all over. Even getting out of bed is hard work. It feels like having the flu for a really, really long time. There are also pills every night at home and spinal taps each month. A spinal tap is when they stick a long needle into your back, take fluid out, and put chemo back in. Your back hurts really, really bad after those. This past fall was not good. I had a lot of fevers and colds, which isn't good for me because I'm more susceptible to infections. I've had a lot of reactions to some of the drugs. I'm very allergic to stuff. I get chills and high temperatures, like 106 degrees.

Disbelief
Hope, 12

I was in denial that I had cancer. Even though I was getting chemo, I just couldn't believe it. I thought, "This is going to be some wacky dream that I'm going to wake up from."

It Knows No Bounds
Javlyn, 16

It's hard living with sickle cell. People think that mostly African Americans get it. All races can get it. I feel more depressed than angry because there's nothing I can do about it, except a bone marrow transplant. That's risky and there's no guarantee that it will work. When you're born with sickle cell, the symptoms usually come out later in life. With me, they came out almost immediately because it was so severe. I have pain in my joints, my back, and my legs. Rain really makes me ache, and also dampness and cold. It's very painful, a stabbing pain like someone's attacking you. I have pain

sick-le cell a-ne-mi-a: a disease that causes red blood cells to change shape, which creates pain and/or clots in blood vessels

every day, and some days are worse than others. I take pain management classes. When it's in my legs, I walk with a limp. I especially feel my legs shaking when I walk downstairs. No one knows if it's gonna get worse as I get older.

Living with Hemophilia
Matthew, 9

Hemophilia is when you're missing a puzzle piece in your blood, and you need a needle stick to put the missing puzzle piece back into your blood—this is how my mom explained it to me. We took a piece of paper and wove 13 other pieces of paper through it, with each piece meaning a blood clotting factor. My mom had me remove the eighth piece, because that's the one missing in me. I said, "Hey, mom, I still got 12!"

Factors eight or nine are the most common ones missing. You can bleed more often, it takes longer to stop the bleeding, and you get more bruises than kids who don't have hemophilia. I don't get bruises and I don't get the bleeds, because I get factor infusions into my blood every other day. We inject the factor into my port, which is in me all the time.

> **blood clot-ting fac-tors (factor):** each factor represents a different protein necessary for blood to clot; normally, a person has 13 factors

Hemophilia is rare in kids. There's no cure. It's genetic. My mom was a carrier, but she didn't know it. When you are a carrier, there's a 50-50 chance that each of your boys will have hemophilia. None of my mom's brothers got it, but my brother and I did.

There are three levels of severity: mild, moderate, and severe, depending on how much of each factor you have in your body. Mine is severe, which means my eight factor level is less than one. The normal range of a factor is 100 to 150. We try to keep my brother and me in the mild to moderate range. We could still have an injury, but we try to be careful. Without factor infusions, we could pretty much bleed to death.

Children in impoverished countries who don't have factor lose limbs or can die. We're very fortunate to be in this country where we have medicine, and we can live pretty normal lives.

I Want a Regular Life
Luke, 22

It's hard sometimes to plan on having a regular life. Should I start going to college for a career, or just get some job that's good? Those are some of the things I think about when I'm alone.

Medical Schmedical
Catyche, 20

Your red blood cells are supposed to be round, but when you don't have a lot of oxygen in your system, your red blood cells become a sickle (banana) shape. They get stuck in the blood vessels and they can pile up, causing a sickle cell crisis. Wherever that pile up is you can be in really bad pain. It will usually hit me all of a sudden. I know the kind that sends me to the hospital, the pain I can't handle at home. Being in the cold, going into a swimming pool that isn't heated, or any form of exercise can really set me off. Sometimes going from air conditioning to humidity, or even stress, can set me off.

I have pain every single day. Most of the time, it's in my back and in my chest. My problem is not the pain alone. It's the fact that I get pneumonia easily because I have a weakened immune system. When I go to the hospital for pneumonia, I have to stay there for weeks at a time. Pneumonia damages my lungs. That's why I'm on oxygen now. I have to use a wheelchair because I can't walk even short distances. I've been on oxygen since I was 12. I even sleep with oxygen.

When I was seven, I had several sickle cell crises, and they found out that I had "acute chest," which is like pneumonia with a lot of chest pain. I was in a coma for seven days. They didn't think I was going to live. They even talked to my mom about unplugging me from the ventilator. My mother wouldn't leave my bedside the entire time. It was really bad for her. I finally woke up.

A Teen's Worst Nightmare
Abbie, 13

Right after my surgery, I started taking steroids and stayed on them through most of my radiation. They were to help keep the brain swelling down while my brain was healing. Steroids make your body retain water, and I gained a lot of weight really quickly. No one told me I'd gain so much weight so quickly. When you do, you get stretch marks on your body. Steroids also cause pimples and some facial hair. As a young lady, none of these are good. Can you imagine a worse nightmare—sudden weight gain, stretch marks, pimples, and facial hair! The weight gain, pimples, and facial hair will all pretty much go away. The stretch marks are there to stay. I watch what I wear now because of the stretch marks.

Seventy-Five Surgeries, and That's Only Part of the Story
Brittney, 15

I've had so many illnesses. I had a kidney transplant when I was one year old. I've been chronically ill most of my life, all related to the kidney transplant. I took 10 pills a day when I was little. Now I take three. I've always had a lot of hospital stays and a lot of doctors' appointments for various illnesses. I've spent half my life in the hospital. On top of that, there are constant appointments for blood work, urine analysis, and the normal childhood illnesses. I got all of the weird childhood illnesses that hardly anyone gets. I had Bordetella, which is kennel cough that dogs get. They say people don't get it. I did. I had psoriasis from the medications, and we had to see dermatologists for that. I've had all kinds of rashes and staph infections.

I've had about 75 surgeries, including the kidney transplant and removing tumors. I got a whole bunch of biopsies. I had a whole lot of central lines and catheters in my stomach and surgeries in my nose and throat. I had PTLD lymphoma (post-transplant lymphoproliferative disorder). It's a cancer and comes from my immune suppressant medications that I had to take so my body would accept my mom's kidney from the transplant. The combination of the immune suppressant medication, and the medicines that I was taking in sixth grade, contributed to me getting the PTLD lymphoma. Then, once, I had fevers of "unknown origin" for over a month. That's all I can think of off the top of my head.

The First Time I Stood
Blayne, 19

I had a doctor come to me one day and say, "We'd like to do a baclofen pump trial on you." That basically means, "We want to stick a big needle into your spine and inject baclofen, and see if it does any good."

bac-lo-fen: a muscle relaxant medication to loosen muscles so they are not so spastic

We did the trial, and I waited six hours for the medicine to take effect. Then they told me to stand up. I had a bunch of physical therapists, my mom, and the doctor standing around me. I felt weak, but I stood and my legs went straight for the first time in my life!

I looked down and started sobbing uncontrollably, because I had never looked so "normal." I was walking up and down the hallway saying, "Look at this!! Mom, look! I have to get a mirror! I want to see me! Somebody take a picture!" I was told that it was going to wear off and the effect was only temporary. I remember turning around and looking at the back of myself going, "Wow!" I gained, like, four inches in height since my legs weren't bowed and crooked anymore.

I felt like I *had* to get this pump installed in my body. It was going to be a hard road, but I definitely had the gumption and wanted to get better. I was 15, and knew that for the first time in my life I had the potential to be cane-less. I jumped at it. They said, "It's going to take a lot of commitment. Are you sure?" I said, "Yes!"

So now I have an intrathecal baclofen pump in my body. It sits underneath my skin to the left of my belly button, and a catheter goes from the pump into my spine. It looks like I swallowed a hockey puck. It pumps baclofen into my blood stream to loosen my muscles so they are not so spastic.

The doctors control the medication being pumped into my spine by a wand through the computer that's in the pump. They have to slowly increase the amount over time as my body adjusts. I'm waiting to see how much better things can get. They have to refill the pump every six to nine months, and they do it with a needle through the port on the front of the pump. Every five to seven years, the battery runs out and I have to replace the whole pump.

When I started the baclofen pump therapy, I had to use two canes to walk. As of two weeks ago, I am now down to no canes! The baclofen pump has really changed my life! I used to never walk out the door without my canes. It took a lot of confidence to know that I was okay without them. It's been strange to learn that I actually have hands available when I'm walking. For the first time I can hold a glass of pop and walk at the same time. It just blows my mind!

At first it was like I had this huge thing sticking out of my left side. I didn't know how to bend or move and I couldn't tie my shoes for the first three months because it got in the way. Some pants don't fit right because of it, and if I lean on a counter, I can feel it. If I want to lie on my stomach, I have to put a pillow underneath it. It's little things like that, but you get used to it.

I recently asked the doctor if it was okay to get a tattoo on my skin over the pump. I wanted something to take away the "Oooohhh" response when people see it the first time. The doctor laughed but called the company that makes the pump and asked them. They said, "Sure, go for it!" Because it's round, I'm thinking probably one of those Greek suns with flames shooting out.

The Hardest Thing My Dad Ever Had to Do
Amber, 15

I had real long, blonde hair down my back, real thick and beautiful. After chemo, hair was everywhere when it started falling out. One morning, I woke up and pushed it back and it fell out in my hands.

I got it cut shoulder length so it wouldn't look so bad falling out. Then one morning, my mama was washing my hair and it was coming out in her hands. That's when I got upset. I said, "Cut it off, Daddy, cut it off, Daddy." My daddy shaved my head and said it was the hardest thing he ever had to do.

I stayed positive. I said, "There's no sense in crying over it because it's gonna come right back." After daddy shaved it off, I was in the bathroom trying on bandanas and making jokes. My parents thought I was crying, but I was making jokes. What else can you do? Crying will only make me feel worse.

> "Just trying to have a good attitude makes it easier on everybody."—*Luke*

Being Told There Is No Hope
Brittney, 15

When I was re-diagnosed, they told us that I wouldn't live. They said, "Even if she responds to the chemo, the next step would be stem cell, and we don't know if she'll make it through stem cell surgery." I didn't want to do the stem cell because I'd have to be in an isolation room and would only be able to visit my friends and family through glass.

I was scared, and I didn't want to be away from my friends. I was crying for hours and hours, because I thought I was being sent home to die. They sent the priest in to talk to me. He said, "You're not going to die." Then the priest started crying, my nurses started crying, and I started crying. My eyes were really sore and red from crying.

I didn't have to do chemo or the stem cell transplant. I'm one of the lucky ones. They can't explain it. The cancer just kinda went away. It's still there, but in a dormant phase right now. It's been a year so far. We've been lucky. I don't have to get regular bone scans anymore; but I have one coming up because I'm having fevers again.

I have emotional ups and downs. I see every day as a blessing, but there is always that uncertainty and not knowing because the cancer could come back. If it does, that's probably when they'll have to do the stem cell transplant. I try to live life to the fullest and keep myself busy so I don't think about it too much.

> "If I'm not healed here, I'll be healed in the hereafter."
> —Jonathan

An Eyesore?
Alan, 20

In our condo, we had a lot of problems putting in an elevator to help me get to our home. We had to build an elevator shaft and a walkway out to it. The homeowner's association did not want it built. They thought it would be an eyesore. I needed it like they needed stairs. We had to sue them, and about two months before going to trial, they agreed to build the elevator. It was a long, expensive process for us, but we prevailed with the help of the Fair Housing Act.

Hair Today, Gone Tomorrow
Hope, 12

The only thing that really made me start bawling was the fact that I was probably going to lose my hair. Hair is very important at my age. Losing it seemed like such a big deal at the time. Now it's like, whatever.

My hair actually hung on for a while. We thought it might just thin, and I wouldn't lose all of it. I got this special shampoo to use that's supposed to help the hair hold on longer, but it still came out in my food, on my pillow, on my shirts, and in my mouth. I could literally take a handful of hair and pull it out and it wouldn't hurt at all.

I'm Not a Racist
Luke, 22

I lost my hair several times. Each time it grew back differently—straight, curly, brown, blonde, and one time even with a bald spot! My dad doesn't even have a bald spot. I'm not gonna have one before he does. It really didn't bother me being bald. I just wore a hat.

In the area where I lived, there were a lot of white supremacists. People assumed I was one of them. I'd say, "No! I have cancer." When I went back for my senior year, people asked, "Why did you shave your head?" They were almost mad at me for doing it. I was like, "I didn't really have a choice. It just fell out."

No Babies
Catyche, 20

I saw a documentary about women with sickle cell who have babies. One woman went into a coma during the birth. She almost died and didn't wake up for several months. That's when it started really hitting me that I cannot have children. I thought I was going to have my career, get married, and have babies. But it's very hard for sickle cell people to have babies because they could die, or lose blood, or have strokes. I would probably die if I had to give birth. That was really hard for me to accept.

I'm thinking about adoption. I always try to think about the future. I read parent magazines all the time. I can't imagine that I can't be pregnant and feel my child kick. I'm going to adopt kids with health issues who no one wants to adopt.

Anger with No End
Faith, 20

At first, I didn't feel angry at my mom about getting HIV from her, but I feel angry now because none of my brothers and sisters got it. I was the last kid born, and it really pisses me off that I'm the only one who has to live with it. I'm mad because there could have been a way to prevent this from happening. Why do I have to be the only one? It hurts to see my sisters getting married and having kids. I'm afraid to have kids because I don't want to infect them.

I Hung On to It Until the Very End
Abbie, 13

When I lost my hair, it was the first time I cried since I was first diagnosed. I didn't cry when they told me I would lose my hair, only when I finally lost it. I was devastated. I was just waiting for the day—and I knew the day was coming.

A guy in radiation told me, "Just shave it off, Abbie. Get it over with." I said, "No!" I kept the last strands hanging on until the very end. I actually had a couple of pieces in the back that wouldn't come out. It was like I was willing them to stay.

I'm wearing a wig now. It's an awesome wig because it looks so natural. It's not hot to wear, and it doesn't make my head itchy. I like it because when I do have hair, it doesn't hurt my hair. I've gone out without my wig. But it took me a while. Now, I'll go outside without a wig or hat and shoot hoops. When friends come over, I'll sometimes not even wear my wig. Most of my friends have seen me without hair.

Dying Sooner Than Later
Aaron, 15

My friend Joyce's cancer is in remission, but we both know it can still come back. Sometimes we talk about dying, but neither one of us is scared. I don't think there is too much to be scared about. You're here in spirit, and heaven is supposed to be such a remarkable and great place. There's not so much we really have to be sad about. There's always the possibility you can die when you walk across the street. Just because it looks like we're going a little bit earlier than expected is no reason to be scared.

Preparing for the Un-Preparable
Amber, 15

They can't save me, you know. I'm not afraid of dying. When it's my time, it's my time. I'll be better off because there'll be no pain and no suffering. I try my best not to worry about the pain. I think about other things as much as I can, happy things, like enjoying my family and friends. I live every day to the fullest.

My doctor assured me that he wouldn't let me suffer, that there was medication for it. We're gonna call hospice when it gets near the end, and stay at home with family and friends. They told me they'd be right there holding my hand, and my puppy will be there. When I get really bad and close to the end, my mom's taking off the last month from work. She's working extra hours now so she can be there with me all the time, which means a lot to me.

> **hos-pice:** a program that provides a caring environment for meeting the physical and emotional needs of the terminally ill

I Want to Be a Kid Again

Catyche, 20

When I was a kid, I always wanted to be older. Now, I want to be younger. I want to go back to a time where I didn't have to depend on myself so much. When you're a kid, everything gets taken care of for you. I want to be taken care of again. It's much easier. If you're a kid and are reading this book, be glad that you have someone taking care of you. Don't be so quick to want to grow up.

Cancer Isn't My Life

Aaron, 15

Cancer isn't my life and it isn't my only problem. It just adds to things. I have a lot of friends and I stay on the phone all night and I have parties. I go out on the weekends to movies, go skating, and go to the mall. Cancer affects my life, but it doesn't change my life. You can't let cancer take control of your life. You have to control the cancer.

I Can't See Color, but I Can Color

Cassidy, 7

I don't have any concept about color, but I like to color. Sometimes I color with markers, which I usually get on my hands. Sometimes I draw a picture of a parachute. They have a special machine that the Lion's Club bought for our school, called a "tracing wheel." You take a picture and put it through the machine, and it makes all the black outlines of the picture rise up so I can feel what to color. We have Braille crayons. They put Braille letters on the crayon to show what the colors are. If it's green, it will say "green" in Braille. I don't know what "green" is. I guess the crayons are for people who weren't born blind.

Some Days, I Just Don't Feel Like It

Ryan, 18

Being in a wheelchair makes bathing challenging and time-consuming. Regular people take it for granted when they jump into a bath or shower. To get into the bathtub, I crawl in like how you would crawl over a wall, or get out of a pool. It gets old. It discourages you from doing what you should. I'm like, "I don't feel like it today, I'm just going to lay here." I don't get like that often, but every once in a while.

The difference between me and you is it takes much longer for me to do daily things. If it takes you 10 minutes to take a shower, it takes me an hour. I don't just sit in there and soak and beautify myself. I'm actually in the tub itself only a couple of minutes. The rest of the time is spent getting in and out.

No Crying!

Miriam, 19

I love to smile, but I didn't smile through all of my treatments. I was strong because I had to be, not because I wanted to. Even to this day, I don't like my parents to see me cry. I go to my friend's house to cry. The only person who knew I was upset was my brother. He knew how I felt without exchanging words. I never cried in front of him either. I don't know why I'm crying now while I'm talking about it. It hurts so badly when I talk about it because it's opening wounds.

It's All Relative

Meredith, 10

I usually have a pretty good attitude, except when I have a "pity party" and feel sorry for myself. One day, we went to my doctor for a checkup. There was a child there who was confined to a wheelchair and couldn't talk. On the way home, I told my mama, "You know mama, we really are blessed. My life is pretty good."

Bouncing Back

Alan, 20

I'm just starting to talk. About six months ago, I started voicing, so now I'm in speech therapy. They put a palette lift (it's like a retainer) in my mouth, so it strengthens my palette so I can talk. I can think it, I can spell it, and I can write it. I know what I want to say, but the pathway is not there. I'm saying words like "mom" and "want" and some of the easier words that begin with "w" or "m." I can say "hi" and "I," and I'm starting to differentiate between vowels and consonants. We're very hopeful that I will be talking in two years.

Some medical professionals never thought that I would be able to walk or talk or eat. Intellectually, I've never lost it, but no one knew for the first year and a half after the suicide attempt what I was really able to do. I'm improving steadily. Usually, you don't improve very much after the first year, but I've improved a lot. They didn't think I would be able to eat because they didn't think I would be able to swallow. I feed myself a little, but I'm messy. One of our goals is to get me to be able to feed myself. Right now, I can eat things like steak that are easy to spear and eat, but soup is another story. I can swallow fine now. It's just gotten better and better. I can eat anything, even popcorn. Water is the last thing that you have to swallow well without aspirating and choking. I've also jumped that hurdle!

Blind and Getting Dressed
Cassidy, 7

I dress myself. For my clothes, I know the front and back because of where the label is. The label goes in the back and I just feel where it is. My mom puts my clothes out for me since I can't see what should go with what. I do everything by myself, except my hair. And someone has to put toothpaste on my brush, or I'll do a big glob.

But It's Finger Therapy
Scotty, 11

Since my relapse, my hands pretty much don't work any more. I can move them, but not pick up stuff. I can't feed myself—that was kinda weird. Also, having your mom brush your teeth is never fun. I told her not to become a dentist. Because of the constriction of my muscles from the MS, my fingers were bent back so far that I couldn't straighten them out. I found my own finger therapy—video games. I tell my mom I play for therapy.

Mitey Riders
Lindsey, 10

I do therapeutic horseback riding at a wonderful farm called Misty Meadows. We're called the Mitey Riders. Horse riding really helps with muscle control and balance. I love it! I have a horse that I ride all the time—not one I own, but that I ride. Her name is Peaches, and she's a palomino, saddle bred. I have a leader who leads the horse on the reins. I don't really need that, I can control the horse myself, but they don't like to take chances. I've been riding since I was four. I'm going to be in a horse show where we show off what we've learned throughout the year.

The Rug as My Guide
Cassidy, 7

Since I'm blind, we have little ways of helping me find my way around our house. At the top of the stairs, we put a rug for me to know that the stairs are ahead. In front of doors there are no rugs so I know I will be entering a room. One day, my mom was vacuuming and moved the rug temporarily. I came along wanting to go into the bathroom. I stepped onto the rug and thought that's where the stairs were. I go to the next doorway where there was no rug, and I stepped in thinking it was the bathroom. It was the stairway, and I fell all the way down to the bottom of the steps. I rolled all the way down, and landed on my back. Luckily, I was just bruised and didn't break anything.

My Brain Felt Like Jell-O
Elyse, 13

I've had my head opened up three times for brain surgery. On the accident date, they took out bone from my head because of the swelling. Then a few hours later, they had to open up the other side of my head. It was something about the pressure. Then they put the bone back in and instead of hardening, it was disintegrating. I could touch my head and it would push in, and it felt like Jell-O.

> "A lot of people don't realize how many parts of their body they move when they walk. I have discovered all of those parts."
> —*Elyse*

Then they opened up my head and put in a plastic thing so it's not like Jell-O anymore. I wanted metal so I would set off alarms at the airport. Also, think of the fashion accessories! I could put magnets on my head. That would be cool! But they don't do metal anymore.

A Way of Life
Luke, 22

When we first found out that I had cancer, I did chemo for 10 weeks and then radiation for several months. I was in remission for almost a year, then it came back—the same cancer in the same place. It's all in my chest, which is why I get worn out so easily. I did chemotherapy again for another six months. I had a few months off and then the cancer came back again. We did a stem cell transplant that time using my own blood.

The cancer came back again after the stem cell transplant. More chemo, then I was healthy for a year. Then my red blood cell count dropped, and my hemoglobin dropped to where I couldn't stand or get out of bed. They didn't know what it was. For months, they were trying to figure it out while I was getting blood transfusions several times a week just to be able to move.

Now, I take a lot of pills and medicine every day. I'm on blood thinners because I get a lot of blood clots. I'm on penicillin since I don't have a spleen any more. I need a bone marrow transplant but they haven't found a match for me yet. With my most recent bout with low blood counts, there were times when I couldn't walk and had to be wheeled around. The biggest thing with me is that I get fatigued, and it really gets frustrating. It's just all of the things I have to deal with, and I do. It's just my life.

Bone Marrow Transplant
Aaron, 15

I just started radiation for my leukemia. They do radiation from my neck down, my whole body. They're preparing me for the bone marrow transplant, and they're killing all the cancer cells.

I'm getting the transplant next week. I have a marrow donor who I haven't met. Bone marrow is a jelly-like substance in the center part of the bone. They put the donor to sleep, and put a needle through the bone into the center part and extract it. The donor may have a little pain, but will feel fine in two days.

A bone marrow transplant is not painful. It's given through an IV, like getting a blood transfusion. The bone marrow is so smart that it knows where to go in your body. The actual transplant is anticlimactic because you're preparing and preparing with the chemo and radiation, which gets you very weak and nauseated, and all your hair falls out.

After the transplant, I'm going to be very weak and I can get infections easily. So the day I get the transplant, my door will be closed, and the only person who can come see me is my mom. She will have to wear a mask and gloves when she comes into my room. I'll be in the hospital on a special floor for transplants for about eight weeks. I can't share my room with anyone because I'll be so susceptible to infections.

Mask of Horror
Abbie, 13

My worst experience was the radiation before chemo. I had to wear this mask that blocks the radiation from going to certain places where they don't want it to go. The mask made me look like some freak in a horror movie.

They made the mask by heating plastic to soften it and form-fit it around my face. It was the longest three and a half hours of my life!

Then for the radiation, I had to lie on this table on my stomach, and they had to clamp my head down so I couldn't move it. You have to lie perfectly still. The radiation was every day and lasted about 20 minutes. I had radiation on my head and spine for the first half, then in the area of the tumor for the second half. After radiation, I had to go through chemo. My chemo treatments were three weeks on and three weeks off. The chemo mostly just made me tired.

I was about 108 pounds before I was diagnosed. My brother used to call me "the beast" because I was muscular and athletic and I played every sport there was except soccer. After chemo, I lost 18 pounds, which is a lot for me. Also, because of the medication I'm on right now, I don't have any reflexes from the knees down. I've been told my reflexes will come back after the treatments are over.

Even the Nurses Were Scared
Charon, 18

The plan was 8 to 12 months of chemo to shrink my tumor, and then do surgery on my leg. They didn't say surgery for amputation, because they didn't know at the time.

The doctor just said he was going to go in and cut out the tumor and replace my bones with rods or whatever.

A lot of the chemo treatments hadn't been working as much as they wanted. When they opened me up for my operation, they saw that the tumor was still growing and spreading, and too big to leave me with my leg. They had to cut off my entire left leg to try and stop the cancer from spreading anywhere else in my body.

I was 17 and strong when I went into surgery. I was ready to get it all over with. But I was mad. Not mad at anybody—just mad. When I got out of surgery, I wasn't in pain. I opened up my eyes, and I felt down where my leg used to be, and I freaked out. It was just the shock—the reality of it. I had a lot of "phantom pain." It felt like my leg was still there and that they were sticking needles in it.

I had one really painful moment after the amputation. It was late at night. They wanted me to get my feeling back, so they took me off the medicine. I started yelling like crazy because I was really hurting. They could hear me all the way to the nurses' station. Even the nurses were scared. But I just needed to get it all out.

After my leg surgery, I had a good summer. I was ready to start back to school for my senior year. I hadn't been to school in a year. I was in school for about a month when I had my routine CAT scan, and the doctor found four tumors in my lungs. I said, "Man, I just grew my hair back!" Again, the chemo wasn't working. You talk about pain—they removed half of my right lung and cut the tumors out of my left lung.

A Chest Full of Stories
Justin, 12

I've had too many surgeries to count. Every now and then, I count the scars on my chest. There were times over the years when the pain was so bad that I didn't think I could go on anymore. There were days when I would be just devastated and wanted to drop over and die. My whole body was changed. I had to learn how to swing on a swing again, and to ride a bike. The drugs I had been given gave me neurological shakes and knocked my balance off. I was very swollen and I'd trip and fall a lot, including down the stairs. That really hurt! But I kept hanging in there.

My problems started when I was born. I immediately turned purple and stopped breathing. After a bunch of tests, they figured out that I had a tiny hole in my heart. They said it would probably close by itself, but it never did. It kept getting bigger over the years, most likely from all the chemo and radiation treatments. I had open-heart surgery when I was 10. I knew that it was a lot more serious surgery than the other surgeries that I'd had. When I got out of the hospital, I couldn't wrestle with my brother. I couldn't jump on the trampoline. I couldn't ride my bike. I could walk and ride in the car—that was it.

All of the treatments at first had been for leukemia. After relapsing with acute myelogenous leukemia (AML), we had to do a bone marrow transplant, and the doctors said it would give me only a 20 percent chance of survival. We had to go to Duke University in North Carolina for the transplant. Our whole family had to move all the way across the country for six months. At Duke, they did a million tests and checked everything, including organ function. Then they put in two ports, one on each side of my body. In preparation for the transplant, they radiated my whole body to totally wipe out my immune system. For six months before the transplant, I received chemo.

Right now, I'm okay. I have to get blood work and scans every six months. Every once in a while, we get a scare—there's a lump or a fever or too many bruises. I'm not really worried about it coming back; I don't think about it. But I do play it up if I'm feeling sick. They said that if we did chemotherapy again, I'd have zero chance of staying alive. I might be around for a few more months, but that's all.

83-Year-Old-Therapist
Blayne, 19

I had a physical therapist from the time I was three months old to age 14. She was Swedish, very old, smoked like a chimney, and was built like a linebacker. This woman was as tough as nails. She'd push me onto the floor and say, "Good job," or "Let's try that again." She was teaching me how to fall. Because of her, I've never even sprained an ankle because I know how to fall. Nobody rates next to her.

She was the one who taught me that I didn't have to be babied. She said "They're starting to do research and finding out that there's a 'helpless complex.' That basically means, if you treat your child like he's helpless, he *will* be helpless. If you treat him like he's capable, he *will* be capable." She always treated me like I was capable. From the start, she taught me to be the best I can be. She's been such an inspiration to me.

Back from the Dead, More Than Once
Tonya, 20

I had four heart attacks in the first weeks of my life. I actually died and came back to life four times. Once, my heart stopped beating for two minutes—the doctors pronounced me dead. My mama got mad when the doctor told her that there was nothing they could do for me. She told the doctor to go back in there and bring me back. They told my mama I'd never live past two, and now I'm 20.

Living with Spina Bifida
Lindsey, 10

Spina bifida is when you have a hole in your spine on the inside of your body. The first month of pregnancy is when the neural tube zips up from the brain to the tailbone, and sometimes it doesn't zip completely. It's like feeding yarn through a straw that has a hole in it—there's going to be a part of the yarn that bulges out. The location of the opening in the spine determines which nerves are damaged. Kids with spina bifida are born with part of the spinal chord exposed; mine is between lumbar vertebrae three and four.

Most kids with spina bifida have to be shunted, which is a surgery performed to relieve pressure inside the skull caused by fluid on the brain. The fluid is drawn off from the brain into the abdominal cavity. A shunt usually has to be

shunt: a tube connecting two locations inside the body to allow for fluids to flow between them

changed as the child grows because it can get infected. Most people who have spina bifida can feel their legs but can't feel their feet. The nerves to their feet are damaged. Some people can walk using hard, plastic braces that keep their feet straight.

I do physical therapy to strengthen my legs so it's easier to walk and my hamstrings won't get tight. To get around I mostly use a wheelchair. I can walk without a wheelchair, if I wear my full braces and use my crutches. If I didn't have leg braces, I couldn't walk because my feet would just flop around. The braces keep them straight. Because of the nerve damage, I can't feel when I have to go to the bathroom, so I have to do something called "cathing." Every four hours I urinate through a tube to keep my bladder empty so bacteria doesn't build up. It's not something I'll ever grow out of because I'll probably never be able to feel.

Like the Game "Operation"
Ryan, 18

Cerebral palsy is like holding onto something so hard that you are just shaking or shuddering from holding on so tight.

I've had two surgeries on my back to help make me less spastic, and to not tighten up so much. In the surgery they cut open your back, go into your lumbar spine, open up your spinal casing, and test your nerves and your spinal cord for spasticity. It reminded me of the game "Operation," where they have this little probe and put it in there to test the nerve endings to see if they were spastic or not. If they met a certain criteria, they cut those nerves and they never grow back, or sometimes they remove them completely. It loosens you up. Before the surgery, I was clinching all the time and had a constant headache. After the surgery, I told my mom, "I don't have a headache today." She said, "Ryan, I am really glad for you." But she didn't get it. I had had a headache all my life. I didn't know what it was like to *not* have a headache. I thought headache pain was normal.

My New Nose
Cassidy, 7

I was born without a nose, and I'm excited about getting my new nose. Why should everybody else have a nose except me? To build a nose, they will use a rib bone so they can attach it to the bone on my face, and it would get a blood supply and grow. But I have to wait until I go through puberty because that's when your bones go through a huge growth spurt, and I could end up with a really big, weird nose. I might wait until I'm 18, just to be on the safe side. When I'm full grown, it will look like everyone else's nose.

A Life and Death Decision
Jonathan, 21

I was going to have surgery to straighten my back because I was curved over. They were going to put Herrington rods in my back so I could sit up straight. During the preliminary exam before the surgery, they found out that my heart was working at one-fourth of what it should be. They gave me medication that helped, but right before the surgery the doctor told me that if my heart stopped during the surgery, they wouldn't be able to revive me and I would die. I had to decide if I wanted to go through with it and risk my heart stopping.

I was 16 and I really wanted to sit up straight like everyone else, so I was willing to take the risk. During the surgery, my heart was having problems. The doctors didn't think I was going to make it. Near the end of the surgery, the doctor came out and told my parents that something weird had happened—my heart began pumping at full capacity. I've been sitting up straight ever since.

It All Led Up to Becoming a Lab Rat
Marian, 16

The doctors don't know why I got juvenile rheumatoid arthritis. They think maybe it was environmental factors, but they really don't know. I'll probably have it for the rest of my life. My systemic form has different symptoms than the other arthritis, like fever, rashes, and a swollen spleen and liver. For a while, I was getting really bad headaches daily. Every morning, my joints stiffen up and I'm stiff for an hour. I always feel pain when I wake up in the morning. It hurts to walk. Sometimes after I stay up late, I get a rash on my hands. Yesterday, I hurt a lot behind my knees. A week ago, I had so much pain in my neck that I was crying. It just comes up in random spots, and then it disappears.

My arthritis symptoms have gotten worse recently; this is the first year I've had injections. The doctor has injected my wrists, my foot, my knees, and my fingers with steroids. It's not good to have injections all the time because steroids wear on the tissue around the joints. At a conference for dermatologists, I was a specimen for them to look at. I sat for two hours as each one looked at my skin rashes. I did not like being their lab rat as they poked around in my skin. In the end, they had many different remedies for me to try. It was scary, all of the cures they had in mind.

Top of the List
Nadia, 12

Children are automatically put at the top of the waiting list to receive kidneys, as long as they meet the blood type. Every time an organ becomes available, they call four people and tell them they are in line first, second, third, or fourth. When I got my first kidney, I was the third in line, but the first two people were sick so I got the kidney. If you have even a common cold, they won't do the surgery because it can be bad for you. I got that kidney, but it failed, and they had to take it back out. I've been at the top of the list again for four years now.

I'm Cancer-Free

Mason, 16

The doctors didn't know how extensive my surgery would be to remove the tumor in my leg. I ended up having a total knee replacement—they removed 12 centimeters down of my tibia and three up of my femur. The surgery took eight and a half hours. I had three different kinds of chemo for two months before the surgery, and for six months after.

After the surgery, I woke up celebrating with the biggest smile on my face. I said, "My cancer is gone!" It had been cut out of my body. Even though I had six months of chemo to go through just to make sure, I knew I was cancer-free and it was a successful operation. There was no doubt about that. The chemo to come was just to ensure that there were no cancer cells left. When they did the surgery, they didn't expect to find it anywhere else, and didn't.

They attached a muscle flap from my calf muscle over some of the metal replacements, and did a skin graft over that. They ran rods up and down my leg to replace the bone, and for support. I have a huge scar where they did the surgery. The scar won't ever go away, the skin will never get thicker, and hair will never grow there.

Now, every six weeks I get x-rays, and every three months I get a bone scan and CAT scan, to make sure the cancer is completely gone. I'm always nervous when I go in, but so far everything has been clear!

The Old Comb-Over

Brittney, 15

When my hair fell out, I was in the eighth grade. Ohhhh, that was hard! It was right around Halloween. I had beautiful, long, curly ringlet hair. I was in the hospital and I was messing around saying, "Wouldn't it be funny if my hair started falling out now?" I got in the shower and a whole clump came out in my hand and it just kept coming out.

My friend was having a Halloween party and I went. We cut my hair short that day. By that night there were a whole bunch of bald spots. I was freaking out. So my mom sprayed my scalp with black hair spray. We tried to fluff up what was left. The day after Halloween I only had a couple of strands left. The rest had fallen out in my bed overnight. I was like, "Mom, if you don't shave the rest of it off, then I will." She was crying while she was shaving my head. I wasn't crying. I looked like a little old man who's totally bald and has like a few wispy hairs at the bottom. We tried the comb-over. My mom wanted to take a picture. I yelled, "No!"

Get a Hat
Miriam, 19

I was a typical 14-year-old. I was very vain, and I lost my hair in a week with the chemo. When I knew it was going to fall out, I pulled it out myself because I didn't want the chemo to take it. Every single hair on my body was gone.

My hair was dead straight and I hated it—until I lost it. But, hey, hair is hair. It's going to grow back. It grows back better. It actually came back blonde! It came back with such life and so much bounce, I actually was happy that I lost my hair. It stayed blonde for three months before turning dark. It's still curlier than it used to be. I know how it is. Losing your hair sucks. Your head gets cold, but get a hat.

Hair Loss Is Better Than Death
Aaron, 15

When they first told me I probably would lose my hair because of chemo, I thought I was going to die—for a girl, that's the worst. I cried. But losing your hair is the least of your problems. Hair will come back. My hair grew back and was really curly, everybody loved it. I liked the way it looked. I actually liked not having hair. You don't have to worry about washing or drying your hair, or putting it up. You don't have to worry about a "bad hair day."

Gee, Thanks!
Hope, 12

One day we were at the doctor's office getting a checkup. I had just started to lose my hair. If you touched it, only a few strands would come out. Dr. McMahan comes in, tousles my hair roughly, and unexpectedly pulls out this huge clump of hair. He just looks at it in shock and tries to put it back on my head. I said, "Gee thanks, what do you want me to do with it now?" The look on his face was so funny.

My Parents Were Worse Than Me

Ivy, 11

When my hair fell out, it didn't bother me. I was sad at first, but I knew it would come back. I had long, dark hair. My parents were fighting over who had to cut it. Neither of them wanted to cut my hair. They finally took me to a salon. The lady who did my haircut was crying while she was cutting it. She kept saying, "You're sure?"

I felt better because my parents shaved their heads, too. My aunt had long, thick, black hair, and even she cut her hair. Everyone shaved their heads for me. That really made me feel better.

Rain on My Head

Jessica, 12

Before I got chemo, they told me that my hair would probably fall out. It started coming out in thin strands, then one night my hair started coming out in chunks. I tried to brush it and my brush was full of hair. We had a party with my cousins, my aunt, and my uncle; and we all shaved our heads together.

I have a perfectly round head, perfect to be bald, but I wore hats in the beginning. When it rained, I'd take my hat off and go stand in the rain. I loved the feeling of the hard rain on my bald head. When it's hailing, I'd run out and stand in it. The hail hurt, but I liked it anyway.

Encouraging Words

Amber, 15

People are always coming up to me and saying, "Amber, I'm keeping you in my prayers." I've heard that about a thousand times. People just don't know how much I appreciate it. It really helps me knowing that I'm being thought about a lot.

Chapter 4

Adventures in School

"A lot of people are scared about dying. My worst fear was missing school."—Aaron

"I want to say God bless to everyone who helps kids like us."—José

"What's interesting is that children ask, 'What happened to you?' and adults ask, 'What's wrong with you?'"—Lindsey

---

Everyone has stories about school, but our stories are about all those things that normal children never have to worry about—uncooperative bathrooms, wheelchair ramps that are too steep (or nonexistent), wearing hats to cover bald heads, taking meds, running over toes with wheelchairs. Oh, yeah, and things all kids have to deal with—riding the bus, cafeteria food, mean kids, and great teachers and bad teachers. You think you've got school stories? Wait until you hear these!

The Sheriff's Son Wore Big Sneakers
Ryan, 18

I was 11 and had just gotten my wheelchair. No one had given me any training on maneuvering, and I wasn't that great of a driver. An 11-year-old kid with a motorized wheelchair and no training is an accident waiting to happen. Now this one kid was a bully, probably because he was the sheriff's son. So with my not-so-good driving skills and his pushy personality, something was bound to happen.

I think I caught the edge of his sneaker under my back wheel. I thought it was just a rock or something, so I go on my happy little way. Oh, he blew up. "You just ran over my foot! You're going to go to jail! I'm going to arrest you. My daddy's going to take you to prison!" I go, "Oh, man, I'm sorry, I didn't mean it." I go on my way to class.

Halfway through class, I hear his name and my name over the intercom to report to the office. I thought that my mom was here to pick me up. I get to the office and they confront me, all of them glaring at me like I did something bad on purpose. The kid was insisting they take him to the emergency room. He was screaming to high heaven, "My leg is broken! The bones are fractured! I'm in so much pain!" I had no idea it was because of me. I just thought he happened to be in there at the same time because he got really hurt somewhere on school grounds.

When our parents got there, we all had a meeting. He sat across from me and just scowled at me like, "I'm going to get you." It finally hit me why we were there. He wore big, bulky, rubberized shoes. I didn't think it could hurt that bad. Fortunately, everyone figured out what was going on with me *accidentally* running over his foot, and they let me go. He was still screaming as I was heading back to class.

Cancer Is NOT Contagious
Sarah, 11

I was bald and wearing a bandana when I went back to school. Most of the kids knew I was bald because of cancer. In gym class we had to hold hands to learn how to square dance. I tried to hold this boy's hand next to me and he blurted out, "I don't want to hold her hand because she has a disease. I want to get another partner." It made me feel really bad and uncomfortable. He was a troublemaker and always tried to make people feel bad. I told him I wasn't contagious. He got in trouble. He never went near me again, which I was glad about.

I'm a Bigger Fan of Me Now

Charon, 18

I'm not the same person since my cancer. Last school year, they had a new rule where kids had to start tucking in their shirts. The kids didn't like it. They said to the teachers, "Just wait till Charon gets back 'cause he ain't gonna do none of that. He ain't gonna listen to none of ya'll."

But now they see I've changed. I'm not talking back to teachers any more. I'm doing my work. I don't really talk to my friends from before. I see the way they get in trouble. I was getting in trouble in tenth grade. They're still getting in trouble the same way in the twelfth grade. I mean, really stupid things, like what I was doing.

For example, you're not supposed to drink soda on carpeted areas. When the principal told them to get off the carpet to drink their soda, they went to the edge of the carpet, but held their sodas over the carpet. If this was back before my cancer, I'd be doing the same thing, and leading the way. But now I see how stupid that kind of stuff is. I don't hang out with them anymore. I know they look at me differently, like I can't keep up with them 'cause I got my leg amputated. And I look at them differently because I think they do stupid things and aren't going anywhere.

I had a lot of bad experiences with teachers back in the day. I argued with every teacher in the school. But now, I've made up with all of the teachers. Before cancer, I didn't care about schoolwork. I felt like, "Nobody's gonna tell me nothing. I'm the 'man' in this school." But now I'm a way better person than I used to be. I have goals now. One goal is to learn to walk with my prosthetic leg 'cause I want to go to the prom. I have a date with a real pretty girl. Losing my leg hasn't slowed me down with the girls. I thought it would, but a lot of people just fall in love with me now when I tell them I have cancer.

I'm Not Breakable

Lindsey, 10

Sometimes I get special privileges that I don't want. Like in our after-school program, there's this teacher who always treats us like we're breakable. All of the other teachers know that I don't need help at all. But this one teacher is shocked every time somebody falls out of their wheelchair or gets hurt in the wheelchair. If we're outside in the winter, she'll be like, "You can go inside anytime you want. I know you'll get cold because you can't move around as much." I don't like that. My wheelchair is practically legs, and I can run in my wheelchair. She practically forces me to be more handicapped. She should just trust me because I know my limitations. I know what I can't do. I don't need a ton of special privileges. I wish she would just treat me normal.

My Teacher Freaked Out

Blayne, 19

The only time that seizures really bugged me was in school. After a while, I got really good about knowing when they were coming. I can't explain how. I just felt this weird thing in my brain and I would know that I was going to have a seizure. This one time in high school, I felt it coming on. I went to my teacher and said, "Look, I don't want to scare you but I think I'm gonna have a seizure."

She freaked and was saying, "What am I supposed to do? Do you need to lie down?" I'm going, "You're the teacher, aren't you supposed to be trained for this?" I'm the kid and she's the teacher, and I have to calm her down, while I feel a seizure coming on! A lot of teachers just went beserk.

Once I remember telling the teacher, "Please call the nurse." By the time the nurse came, I wasn't thinking clearly. The nurse said to me, "Blayne, do you want to go home?" I'm a dedicated student, I pulled a 3.9 when I graduated high school. I hadn't missed a day in five years. I'm not going home. She said, "Blayne, if you're going to have a seizure, you need to go home." I said, "Well, I'm not gonna." She gave me a pillow and literally propped me up in the corner of the room and went to call my mom. My mom was going to take me home whether I wanted to go or not.

> **sei·zure:** sudden and abnormal electrical discharges in the brain that cause shaking, loss of consciousness, or other physical symptoms

My mom's on her way, and they wanted to get me out of the classroom. They get me walking to the office. As I'm walking, I looked at her and I said, "Here it comes." She's like, "Well, sit down." I'm standing. She's like, "Blayne SIT DOWN!" She actually kicked the back of my knees out from under me, and laid me down on the concrete right in the middle of the school's atrium. While I was having the seizure, school let out. A thousand kids were all around me, but the teachers were awesome in respecting my privacy.

They got in a circle around me and none of the kids could see a thing. It was really great. They had the assistant principal in the circle—this suit-and-tie guy with nice, expensive shoes. While I was having the seizure, I grabbed his foot and put my head on it, and I was drooling on his shoe! I remember waking up and looking at this guy's shoe and was so embarrassed. He just says, "Hey, it's part of life." I remember apologizing to him profusely thinking, "I'm never going to be able to look him in the eye again." But people move on and nobody remembers.

Really, I'm Not that Lucky
Justin, 12

I miss a lot of school for being fatigued and having lots of pain. I had to explain to the kids at school why I missed so much school. They're always saying, "Oh, man, you're so lucky." I'm like, "No, I'm not! I'd much rather be in school!" Sometimes, they ask me silly questions, like if I'm contagious. I just sort of giggle and say, "No, it's very much not contagious." As much as I try to explain to them, a lot of the kids still say, "Man, you're so lucky 'cause you're almost never here for school." I say, "I'd much rather be here than sick at home."

I'm Smart, but I Can't Write or Read
Tonya, 20

I've never been to school. I don't know how to write or read. The school people said that I was going to die anyway, like real young, so why bother teaching me anything? They actually said that. Once, these people came from the state board of education. They saw me and my condition, and looked at my medical records. They said no public school for me because I wasn't well enough. They told us to try homeschooling and hopefully that would work. They sent folks from the local school a couple of times to work with me. But I couldn't keep up. They finally said, "Just forget it."

My mama really doesn't want me going to school. If I went to school, everyone would make fun of me. It hurts me real bad when kids make fun of me. Do they think that just because I'm in a wheelchair, I don't have feelings? My mama took me to another school, and they were going to try to get me enrolled there in a special class. They found out that I had a bad breathing problem, and they didn't want to be responsible if I quit breathing and died.

Well, I've lived, and now I can't read or write.

Blame the Elephant
Blayne, 19

I don't mind explaining my situation to adults, but kids my age, I mess with them. When I was eight, I got tired of answering all the questions about my situation. I told a kid I worked in the circus and that an elephant had sat on me. He was like, "No way!" I said, "Yeah, my mom still works trapeze." He believed me, and the whole school thought I was cool.

Quit Stealing My Wheelchair
Lindsey, 10

I've had people try to steal my wheelchair on the playground. I'll get out of my wheelchair to sit on a swing and someone is either sitting in my wheelchair or rolling it around. All of the kids want to get into my wheelchair. The first day of school, people actually fought over my wheelchair to push me. I ended up having a different person push me every two days for the entire school year.

Usually, I have to remind people, "I'm not a plaything, and my wheelchair is a piece of working equipment and not a toy." One day after school, I was sitting reading a book. This girl had people lined up waiting to take a spin in my wheelchair. They were ramming into walls on purpose. I was so mad at her. I think of my wheelchair as my legs. I was like, "You don't understand, it's like cutting someone's legs off."

My Principal Said, "Pee in a Cup"
Jonathan, 21

I was about 14, and couldn't use the bathrooms in my school. They just weren't accessible to me in my wheelchair, even though, by law, they were supposed to be. They had just regular bathrooms that were too narrow for my wheelchair. I was too scared to bring it up to anyone. So I wouldn't drink anything for breakfast or lunch. I'd hold it all day, and wait until I could get home where I could use a bathroom. Then one day, I had an accident. I went home and tried to clean myself up, and then my dad asked me what happened. I told him that I couldn't hold it any more. My dad got upset, and the next day he dropped me off at my school and went into the bathroom to see for himself.

People think that since the American Disabilities Act was passed in 1990—making laws about public areas being accessible to everyone—everything is okay. But my public school wasn't following the laws. The only thing they had was a ramp to go up to the stage in the media center since I was in concert band. But the ramp was so steep that even my parents had difficulty getting me onto the stage.

My parents and I met with the IEP (Individual Education Program) committee and some of the school administrators. We all walked around the school and saw all the problems. The committee members were making different recommendations. The principal said, "We can take the teachers' lounge and use that lounge and that bathroom for Jonathan." He would deprive the teachers of their lounge for me.

They were all getting upset because they didn't know what to do. It was embarrassing—most people never have to think about these things. We were having this whole big thing, just so I could go to the bathroom at school like the other kids. Finally, my dad said, "May I give you a suggestion? You have just built a million-dollar library with a spacious bathroom. Put some strips on the floor and get him a urinal." They actually said they couldn't get a urinal but they could get a cup for me to use. That was their solution—for me to pee into a cup instead of using a bathroom! Finally, my parents bought two hand-held urinals, and then someone helped me twice a day.

I Can't Kick the Boys Anymore
Elyse, 13

School is different after the car accident. I can't kick boys anymore without losing my balance. Some of the kids treat me differently. I don't know if it is related to the accident, but the new kids who didn't know me before the accident seem more friendly to me. They come over and sit by me at lunch and hang out with me. They all take turns grabbing onto my hand to help me walk.

My mom goes with me to school now. I don't need her, but she insists on being in my classes to help me get my stuff out and to write class notes for me, because I now have use of only one hand. It's embarrassing to have an aid, especially my own mother. Most people don't want to do anything that makes them different in school because they want to be like everybody else. I want to be unique and weird. I started the trend of wearing overalls backwards. I'm not afraid to try new ideas.

My Mom Wouldn't Take Me Home
Abbie, 13

I lost all of my hair the summer before the eighth grade. You can't wear hats at school. On the first day of class, I wore a hip-hat—a hat with hair attached to it. Right when I walked into school, the principal, who was new, yelled at me about wearing a hat. I didn't take it off; I just kept on walking. The principal yelled at me, "Come here now!" She took me into another room. I was crying so hard, I could barely get out that I had cancer. She was shocked and felt really bad.

I was afraid of being asked to take off my hat. I wanted to leave school immediately. They called my parents to come get me. My mom came, and I was just hysterical. I was already a nervous wreck going back after losing all my hair. Then she left me there! She refused to take me home. She figured that if she took me home, I would never go back. She told me later it was hard for her to leave me there, but she thought she was doing the right thing.

The fear of being asked to take my hat off had been a constant fear. My mom had been talking to my counselor all summer. Everyone knew about me, except the new principal. We thought everything had been taken care of. I guess you can only cover the bases you know about. Later, the principal actually bought me a new hat.

I Taught a Teacher
Blayne, 19

I ran into this teacher one day; and I just really needed to talk to someone. Her name was Sharon Hippy, and she was exactly that—an old hippy. She was my substitute teacher and I was having a really crappy "Blayne's disabled day." She said, "You know what? Buck up! Blayne, you have no idea what you have taught me. Let me just tell you the things in this hour that you have taught me, just watching you move from your desk to get the stapler, and just do the things that you do. Sitting here watching you for an hour, you have no idea."

She started listing all the things—patience, understanding, compromise—she had seen in me in an hour. I was just speechless. That was five years ago, and I've talked to her once a week ever since.

Suddenly a Stranger
Abbie, 13

There were rumors flying around that I was going to die. My mom was getting calls from teachers and parents saying, "I need to know what to tell these kids. There are so many rumors flying around the school."

My mom and I went to school to pick up something. We were trying to get out of the school before the bell rang to change classes. We missed. Here come all the kids, chitchatting. Then all of a sudden the hall grew quiet. It's like they saw me and shut up. They're so immature, they don't know how to deal with it. And they don't know whether to talk or not say anything. It hurt my feelings. It made me feel different. Three months earlier I was Abbie—now I'm some stranger. My mom keeps telling me, "You will never be one of those people who looks at somebody and makes fun of them, because you've been on the other side of that."

Great Teachers (and a Slack One)
Mason, 16

My teachers were great. They were somewhat lenient on letting me catch up with all the work, so I didn't have to repeat the grade. But they didn't forego the tests or exams. I went to school as often as I could, if my blood counts were all right and if I was feeling all right. But that was extremely rare. I had someone come over from school and help me with math, biology, and history. I'm a pretty good student, and didn't want cancer to slow me down.

> **blood count:** the number of red and white blood cells in your body, and an indicator of illness if an abnormal amount is counted

My parents had to pay for the tutors because I went to a private school. My math tutor was fantastic. She said, "I will not take money. It's not Mason's fault that he cannot come to school. I think that all the teachers should provide for him to catch up." My English teacher went way beyond the call of duty. He came to the hospital just to visit. He was fantastic. Even my report card would say, "Incomplete for now, worry about your health, don't worry about your grades." They were all supportive, except my history teacher. He was not present at all. He was really slack—just what you would accuse students of being—about everything.

The Invisible Problem

Marian, 16

I have a 3.8 GPA, and I'm in honor society. I have to work extra hard to do this. It bothers me because people can stay up doing their homework until midnight, while I have to have my homework done by 9:00 because I just can't do it afterward. I'm so tired and I'm not feeling well by that time. I just want to go to bed. That's what I want people to understand—it's so hard for me to get all my schoolwork done. I'm in really hard classes on top of it.

Some teachers are more understanding than others. Freshman physical education was really hard, and a lot of times I just couldn't do it—all the running and stuff—but sometimes they would still make me run. It was really stressful for me because my grade was affected by it. I'd say, "I can't run. My knee hurts." I don't know if she didn't believe me, because when people can't always see the problem, they don't understand. If I didn't have symptoms that day, but it still hurt, people would say, "Well, you look okay." They just don't believe me. I think it's much easier for kids who have cancer. At least people understand that illness and don't think you're faking it.

Shaving the Janitor's Head

Jessica, 12

People at school knew what was going on with me. My friends were always nice to me. For example, I couldn't run because I had lost the strength in my legs. Instead of running ahead like they did before, they would stay back with me. Some of the younger kids asked silly questions like, "Can I catch this from you?" Some of the kids were mean. At school, I'd wear a hat. Someone tried to take my hat while I was wearing it. That's not nice. Our school is three levels with an elevator. Kids are not allowed to use the elevator—only me and other kids who have reasons to use the elevator. So kids really became "real good buddies" to ride the elevator with me.

They did a school fund-raiser—if you raise this much money, the janitor will do something; if you raise this much more money, he'll dye his hair the brightest pink they can find. If you raise this much money, then he'll shave his head. They raised the highest amount, and I got to shave his head. That was cool.

Respect Me, Don't Overprotect Me
Miriam, 19

I didn't think the people at my school gave me the respect I deserved. During my relapse, I didn't want a wig anymore. I wanted to go with my do-rags, my bandanas, and my hats. Even our security guards, who knew what was going on, told me to take off my hat because it was against school policy to wear one. They sent me to the principal's office because I refused to take off my hat. I got there and started yelling, "How can those security guards tell me to take off my hat when you guys know what's going on?" The principal was like, "I'm sorry." I'm like, "Sorry ain't the word." I told them what to do. While I was sick, I was taught to take control of the situation. Make this work for you—don't make it work against you.

I noticed that my friends were overprotective. They would look at people and tell them to shut up if they started to say anything that they shouldn't say. They sheltered me. They'd come visit me in my house to see how I was feeling, to see how bored I was. Everyone would take me everywhere 'cause they'd look at me and say, "Oh, you poor thing."

> "Everybody has something different about them; but we're all just kids."
> —*Scotty*

Desperately Trying to Fit In
Catyche, 20

There was no physical sign of me being different. I was able to walk normal, and I made sure that there was no appearance that made me different. It was difficult for me to climb stairs, but I never showed anyone that I had problems. I forced myself, even if I couldn't breathe and was about to pass out. I was always afraid that people were talking about me, thinking I'm different, and wouldn't want to be my friend.

Once in the eighth grade, we were going from my middle school to the high school to check out how it was going to be the next year. There was no way I was going to humiliate myself by saying that I couldn't walk that far. I wanted to be just like everyone else and I was going to walk it. After a few blocks, I couldn't breathe; my head was spinning and I couldn't walk any more. It was this huge scene. I was about to pass out. There were a lot of people around, and some people were trying to help me. It was so embarrassing. They brought a rolling office chair over to me. I guess they didn't have a wheelchair. I refused to get into the chair. I think I got to the high school by one person on each arm helping me walk. I don't remember much because when I get like that I don't know what's going on around me.

Don't Walk Over Me
Blayne, 19

Falling is almost an everyday occurrence for me. It always freaks people out. High school, it seems, is just a completely different society than the rest of the world. I'll fall in the middle of the hall while changing classes and literally—I kid you not—kids walk over me and act like I'm not even there. I'm not kidding—people actually step over me. I'm thinking, "Goodness, where are your priorities? You can't even take the time to walk around?" I don't mind if you don't stop and ask me if I need help because, to be honest, I can do it better by myself. There's really an art and technique to helping me up because I weigh so much. People will actually come over and start yanking on all parts of my body—like that helps me get up. So I don't mind people not helping. But to just walk over me? Hello!

Show and Tell
Ryan, 18

At school, whenever we did "show and tell," I was the show and tell. Kids would ask me questions and become a little more aware of my disability. I did that every year. Some of the kids already knew about me, but there are always new kids cycling through so you have to do it again and again each year. It was pretty cool because I also got feedback. I think it helped us all.

Listen Up, Teachers
Lindsey, 10

One day, my teacher had this cool idea. I had this extra wheelchair, and he had me bring it to school. We put everybody's name in this hat except for mine. Every day they'd pull out a name, and the person would have to use the wheelchair the entire day.

They'd have to go to the handicapped bathroom. They could only get out of the wheelchair if they were going to sit on the toilet. They had to push themselves. They couldn't let anybody else push them. They couldn't sit in a regular chair in class. They had to sit in the wheelchair for the entire day, like go through the lunch line in it and everything like that until the end of the day. The teacher actually yelled at them if they got out of the wheelchair. I remember hearing, "I'm glad that's over." By the end of the year, everybody was shocked at how hard it was. It helped them understand what I go through every day.

Feeling Left Out
Miriam, 19

The hardest part about cancer was feeling left out of my circle of friends because I simply couldn't be there. I would get depressed because I wanted to be normal. I wanted to go to my junior prom. I wanted to be there to make fun of my classmates when they did something stupid, not by having my friends call me and tell me what they did or what my classmates did. I didn't want to be left out of the circle. I was upset.

No Special Favors
Aaron, 15

When I came back, I was ready to do schoolwork like everybody else. I didn't want anybody to feel sorry for me. My friends knew that, and they handled it really well. The kids put a poster on my locker that read, "Aaron Casey Is a Survivor." A bunch of kids and teachers signed it.

A lot of teachers would say, "Oh, you can hand in your paper a day late." I didn't like that. I wanted to be treated equally, and I handed in my papers on time. When I went back to school, they sent a paper from the hospital saying that I may need to take a break, or I may need to have a snack, but I didn't need any of that. If I were late, they would say, "Just go to class. It's okay." If I were tired, they would say, "Go to the nurse and lay down." I didn't want to go to the nurse and lay down. If I was tired, it was because I was on the phone all night, not because of my cancer. I'd always say to them, "Don't treat me different! There's nothing these kids can do that I can't."

The Big Performance—Not!
Jonathan, 21

I played clarinet and keyboard in high school, and I was in concert band. I was really excited about a concert we were going to have. My dad asked me, "Jonathan, should we tour the facilities to see if it is accessible for your wheelchair to get on the stage? Remember last time?" I said, "Dad, I already asked them about that, and they told me that everything was fine."

So we go to the high school gym the night of the concert, and we walked around to the back, but we didn't see a ramp. My dad asked the band director if he could tell us where the ramp was. My dad said, "Apparently, we're visually impaired, we cannot find the ramp." The band director said, "It's right back there." He went to show us. But there was no ramp.

I never got to perform that night in the spring concert because they couldn't get my wheelchair on stage without a ramp. I was very disappointed. My parents called a local news reporter. The reporter talked to the school board, the administration, and the teachers, and found out that the school administration was not fully knowledgeable about the American Disabilities Act and the 504 laws. They were supposed to designate a teacher who has a specialty in that area to chair that committee, and they hadn't done that. The reporter took a picture of me in the auditorium, and they had a story about me on the front page of the paper. Finally, some things started happening for the better.

We had this big meeting with the school about facilities for kids in wheelchairs. The room was pretty full. My dad asked them if they had a plan of action for me, like if there was a bomb threat, or the electricity went off, or for a fire. They got upset because my dad challenged them about something they weren't doing. Even the chair of the special education department got very upset. My dad's a special ed teacher in another school, so he knows all about the Americans with Disabilities Act. The special education department and school weren't doing their jobs.

I wasn't the only kid they ever had in a wheelchair. Another kid in a wheelchair had gone through before me, but his mother had done everything for him and didn't ask the school to do anything. She would go to the school four to five times a day to do things for him because she never knew the law. My parents couldn't do that because they were both working. It was a big deal for a while until we finally got everything worked out. After that, I served on the city council for the ADA.

The School Bus
Ryan, 18

I always rode the regular bus. It had a lift on it, and a space in the back where they had taken out a couple of seats. When they came out with the "special" buses, people assumed it was the "retarded bus." Myself and some other kids would tell them to shut up because they didn't know what they were talking about. It's not a wagon full of people who are completely mentally insane. They think that's why the windows are always up on the bus, to hold kids in there.

Blind in School
Cassidy, 7

I'm in regular class for social studies and science. For reading, writing, and math, I go to a different room called VI (Visually Impaired) where we are taught by the Braille teacher. I read way above my level in the second grade. I read all in Braille. I read Braille faster than other kids read regular books.

I also have a class called O&M, where I learn orientation and mobility. Most people, when they walk across a room, go in a straight line. But I don't know if I'm in a straight line, because I can't see. So I usually go off track and run into stuff. O&M teaches me how to find my way around a room. I can't cut across the middle of a room. There is no straight line for me. I have to go around the edges or use counters. O&M teaches how to do "trailing"—running your hand along the wall or a counter to find your way as you walk along. When you get to an open space, like a door, you trail with your foot on the floor until you get to the other side. At school, there are Braille signs on the doors to tell me what classroom is which. I have the school memorized. Someone taught me all the places and I remember where they're at.

My "A-Team" Running Point for Me
Mason, 16

I go to a small school, and word spread pretty quickly that I had cancer. Mom and Dad had a conference with the teachers, and the hospital's Child Life person spoke to everyone at school to prepare them for me coming back. She was really very helpful, and did a really great job talking to everyone. She prepared teachers for the situation that, if they don't see me in school for a week, then see me at a football game on a school night, that's because that's the hour I feel good. Don't think I'm just laying out of school because I didn't come to school that day.

A friend of ours brought the Lance Armstrong yellow "Live Strong" wristbands for everyone in my grade. When I first came back, everyone was wearing them, and most of them wore them for the whole year, which was really cool. The kids at school were all very supportive. No one treated me any differently, which was great. They were really sweet and always asked if they could do anything for me. It wasn't a lot of extra attention. I liked that everyone treated me the same.

Baldy
Autumn, 11

One time, I went to school without any covering on my head. Two boys started picking on me, and I started crying. My friend asked me what was wrong. I told her, and she told our teacher, who then shaved her head for me. She had breast cancer two years before. She brought her port to school and explained to all the kids about cancer and hair loss.

My High School Actually Kicked Me Out
Catyche, 20

I went to a special high school where I'd gotten a scholarship. It was a very intense, rigorous academic experience. I was very good at school, but when I'd get sick it was hard to make it up, especially at that type of school. It's a private school, so they don't send tutors to your home to help you out or give you extensions of time to make things up. They basically wanted me to make up one whole year within another year. So I would be doing two years' worth of work in one year.

What happened was that during my junior year I was in the hospital for a month and my depression started. I struggled through the year trying to make it up. I was absent for long periods of time. We spoke with my teachers, and I begged them to give me a chance to make up my work. They wouldn't give me a break, even based on my past academic excellence. There was no way that I would be able to do two years of work in one year. Then I got sick again, so I now had to do the present senior work, past senior work, and my junior work—all of which I couldn't do because I was really sick.

The school asked for a meeting to see how I could best finish my work and graduate. When we actually had the meeting, they talked about my options—whether I was going to get a GED or go to another high school. They said, "It's not working out. Maybe you should make the decision."

I started crying. I walked into the room expecting one thing, and then they are pushing me to make the decision to leave. My mom was there. I said, "Are you asking me to leave?" They said, "No, we're not asking you to leave." I said, "So I can stay?" They said, "Well, we think you should make the decision not to stay because you realize you won't be able to finish." They refused to ask me to leave, but it was obvious what they wanted. They were trying to push me toward leaving, although they refused to say the words. They were trying to make me say that it was my idea to leave.

My mom and I were both crying and upset. My mom said, "Just sign it. They don't want you. We'll find another place." They had the contract all ready. They were so sure I needed to go. It was just a matter of getting me to agree without suing them. I signed the contract. It was very heartbreaking because that was the school that I really wanted to go to. I went to get my stuff from my locker, and I was thankful that there was no one there because I didn't want to see anyone.

My Teacher Wanted to Sue Me!

Jonathan, 21

In eighth grade, I ran over my teacher's foot with my wheelchair during class. She was standing behind me and I didn't see her as I was backing up. Some of the students laughed because she wasn't a popular teacher. I thought it was funny, too, in a way, because I didn't know she was really hurt. I cracked the bones in the top of her foot, just hairline fractures. She had to use crutches for a while, and she missed a couple of days of work.

She actually wanted to sue me—a 13-year-old. Of course, that meant suing my parents. I got really scared about the lawsuit—and my grade. Fortunately, my parents and the school were able to calm her down and talk her out of it. But, you know, I stayed in her class the whole time, and she never really treated me differently. It was all very strange.

Chapter 5

Hospital Tips and Tales

"In my file, it says **I'm allergic to the hospital."** —Mookie

"Chemo and food don't mix, and **don't ever let them tell you different."** —Amber

"My mom asked if I felt like I was dying, and I said, **'I don't know, I've never died before.'"** —Hope

The hospital can be the most dreadful place on the planet. It's the one place where you'll never get a good night's sleep, and you'll never get used to all those sterile, antiseptic, gross smells. Here are our helpful hints to make your hospital stay more homey—tips for decorating your room and IV pole, how to get better room service, creative ways to pass the time (syringes make great squirt guns), and what to eat and not eat in the hospital (usually never the food). There are even ways to make extra cash in the hospital.

Make Your Room "Alive"
Sarah, 11

Do whatever you can to make your room brighter. One trick we found was with the shiny balloons filled with helium. If people buy them at the hospital gift shop, you can get them refilled for free. Or, once they start to lose their air, you can cut the bottom off and hang them on the wall. They look pretty and colorful.

Get out of your room as much as you can, even if it's just to go down the hallway. If your hospital has a courtyard, or a nice place outside, go there as much as you can. I think sunshine and fresh air are so important. Go to all the activities. Go out and see the therapy dogs, and let the dogs come into your room. Do anything to get out and get your mind off your illness.

The Child Life people would try to talk kids into getting out of their rooms. I'd help get younger kids out of their rooms. Usually they would get out, even if I had to keep asking them. Our hospital had this program called "Starbright World," where you can talk to other kids in different hospitals. It had a little camera so you could see each other and sometimes a microphone. See if your hospital has Starbright World!

Sneak Your Pets into Your Room
Hope, 12

If your pet is small enough, sneak him up to your room. All they can do is yell at you. My mom was so afraid they would throw us out, if they caught us. I said, "Toss me out of the hospital! I don't care." It really lifted my spirits to have my kitten for visits. I went from being under the covers in a depression, to elated and happy. We smuggled my kitten into my hospital room lots of times. We'd just put him into a duffle bag. My cousin Wendy stood guard outside my door. If nurses tried to come in, she'd say, "Don't disturb them. They're having a family moment." Wendy never lied in her life before I went in the hospital.

Get Out and Mingle
Charon, 18

After I started going out of my hospital room, I met new people and they have become good friends. The more people you meet, the more fun you will have. I understand that if you don't feel good, you don't want to leave your room. But if you're depressed, sometimes you have to suck it up and get out and meet people. You're stuck in there until they let you out, and you're not going to get through it by being depressed. If you stay depressed and alone all the time, you won't make it!

Name Your IV—Yeah, Like that Helps
Hope, 12

They say to name your IV pole because it goes everywhere with you, so you're supposed to be friendly with it. It's supposed to be your best friend, but I thought it was a pain. I named it "Lucifer." I hated it being everywhere near me.

Always try to cover your IV pole. Put a pillowcase over it and decorate the pillowcase. Sometimes if you look at the IV fluid, it makes you sick. One of the fluids is red, and it doesn't look very good, and it makes you sick to look at. Lots of people don't like seeing their IV fluid.

Ivy the IV Pole
Amber, 15

Okay, now it's not the best friend you'll ever have, but your IV pole has to go with you everywhere like a friend, so you have to do something with it. You might as well make the best of it. I named my IV pole "Ivy" and put a hat on it. I even dressed it up for Halloween. We put bandages on the pole once, like it had been in a wreck. I think you should name the thing to make fun of it since it's with you all the time, even though you hate it and it's a pain.

My Crafty Room
Autumn, 11

Decorate everything in sight—anything to make your stay better! I decorated my hospital room with pictures and arts and crafts. Everything I made, I'd put on my walls and in my room, along with cards, stuffed animals, and flowers. I'd make collages with pictures out of magazines. I made thank-you cards for the nurses and doctors—they really like that! I had a sign on my door saying, "Autumn's Room." My door was slapped full of pictures and signs. The Child Life people would give us stickers, and I'd put those everywhere. Child Life time was my favorite time. I went to all of their activities.

I'd also tie balloons on my IV pole. We blew up a glove and made it into a cow. Sometimes I'd make glove chickens and put faces on them. When I was smaller, I'd ride the IV pole. I'd stand on the pole and my brother would push me down the hall.

Games, Pillows, and an Important Quilt
Hope, 12

You *have* to bring your own stuff to the hospital. I don't want any hospital sheets on me. My sheets from home were softer and didn't smell like the hospital. Take your own pillow. I wouldn't put my head on a hospital pillow because of the smell. I brought my quilt that my friends made for me. They put all of their handprints on it and the paw prints of my kittens and dog. I take it with me every time I go to the hospital, and I keep it on me when I lay around at home. I make my mom wash all of my blankets and everything when we come home from the hospital. I take a shower, too. The hospital smell just makes you want to puke, even at home if you get a whiff of it from things that have been in the hospital. It's the worst smell in the world.

Try to get your own room if you can. Also, ask about the movies because they always have a lot of movies that you can watch in your room. Sometimes they have electronic games that you can borrow.

You can even get an extra bed. One of my parents always stayed with me every night. It makes a huge difference to know they are there at night.

Pack Cool Stuff
Amber, 15

Make your hospital room as much like home as you can and as comfy as possible—the sky's the limit. When I get there, I'll walk in and start unpacking, and within 30 minutes it looks like my room at home. I always take my "Rainbow of Love" pillowcase and my sheet that my friends decorated for me and signed with their names and messages—I hang that on the hospital room wall where I can see it from bed. I take my favorite blanket, pictures of me and my friends, movies, phone cards, and my laptop computer.

We bring our own snacks and drinks from home. If you go to the cafeteria and buy a drink, it's $1.50. A pack of crackers is $1.00. All that stuff adds up quickly when you're there a lot. They have a refrigerator so you can label your food and put it in there. We took sandwich meat and microwave popcorn.

We bring a foam mat to make the bed softer. You wouldn't believe what a difference that makes! We're "regulars," so the hospital gave us a place to store things.

I Didn't Want It Like Home
Mason, 16

I would always bring a pad and sleep cover to put over the plastic-covered mattress. I brought pillows. I tried not to make it too comfortable because I wanted to get out of there. I told my mom, "I don't want to get used to this. I don't want to make it too comfortable." I didn't decorate my room. I never put anything on the walls. My dad always took the balloons that I'd get to little kids' rooms. I only brought my little stuffed monkey Coco, and my squishy pillow. I made it comfortable enough so that I could actually stay there a couple of nights, then go home. I was always so eager to get out of there. I always felt better as soon as I'd come home.

Bring Only the Fun Stuff
José, 11

When I'm in the hospital, my mom lets me do pretty much what I want and eat what I want—anything to help me get through the long hospital visits. I bring anything that is fun—and nothing that isn't fun. I also paint the window in my room. The last thing I painted was a turtle made out of shapes. Also, whenever anyone would come from "the outside," I'd have them bring me things—mostly food. The food in the hospital is truly the worst on the planet!

Room Reservations, Please
Amber, 15

The night before you're going in, call the hospital and find out what rooms are available. At my hospital, when you get to be a "regular," you can pick the room you want, and they'll try to reserve it for you. Of course, I'd pick the biggest one or the one closest to the nurse's station so I could see all the action.

Put Your Pet on the Ceiling
Scotty, 11

Always have a picture of your favorite pet on the ceiling above your bed. When you are lying in bed, that's always where you are looking, and that's the first thing you see in the morning. Unless the nurse is there leaning over your bed and waking you up, then you see the nurse first, which is never good.

Hospital Rooms Need Themes
Hope, 12

Themes are the best decorations. My family makes my room into a theme every time I go to the hospital. One of the themes was a beach scene. They went to a party store and got palm trees and put them on the wall with streamers and stuff. All the nurses come into my room to see what my theme is for this visit. My cousin Wendy comes in before I'm admitted and decorates my room. We call her the "decorating bandit." We've also had cartoon character themes and a Holden Beach theme, which is where we go for Labor Day and the 4th of July. We even had a Jimmy Buffett theme with parrots hanging down. This way, you're not looking at the four walls of a hospital room.

Be Nice to the Nurses and Get an IV with Good Wheels
Luke, 22

If you're gonna be mean to somebody, take it out on the doctors—you're gonna see the doctors the least. The nurses are always there in the middle of the night if you want somebody to bring you a milkshake or something. So you want them on your side.

With the IV pole, try to get one with good wheels—they are better to ride. The nurses get nervous when you ride your IV, and they get even more nervous when you start building ramps. Also, for older teens, try to stay on the kids' floor as long as you can. You get much better treatment, and it's definitely more fun.

Some of the Best Foods for Bad Taste
Scotty, 11

There is no limit on what to bring. We had lots of food, good snacks like cookies, pretzels, candy, fruit drinks, chicken patties, corn dogs, and chips. The steroids I was on gave the food a metallic taste. To get that taste out of your mouth you've gotta find what food works for you. Baked barbecue chips got rid of the metallic taste for me, and Sunkist and Oreos were some of the only things that actually stayed the same in taste.

Mom didn't really care what I ate. I had lost weight and she was just happy to see me eating. I got to eat all of my favorite foods. We had a refrigerator in the nourishment room down the hall where they had a microwave. We cooked our own stuff, and for good reason—there's mystery meat that they'd bring in. Really, I have no idea what creature that meat came from!

Air Freshener, Who Would Have Thought
Brittney, 15

The smells bothered me. My mom brought me air fresheners and candles. It was such a simple thing that made all the difference in the world.

Mystery Meats and Soggy Chicken
Sarah, 11

I wouldn't even let them bring the food tray into the room because of the smell and look of the food—didn't even get to the tasting part. They'd bring this meat thing with rice, some sort of mystery meat. For lunch there'd be broccoli and chicken fingers. It would sit under the cover and get soggy while it was waiting to be delivered. I don't know anyone who would eat soggy chicken fingers.

The first time I went in, my parents tried to give me healthy foods to help make me healthy. I wouldn't eat any healthy foods. Eventually, my parents let me eat anything I wanted, just so I'd eat. I got on this huge kick for broccoli, peaches, and oatmeal. That's all I'd eat, and I could have eaten anything I wanted, like cookies and ice cream!

> "Don't eat the bran muffins in the hospital. Enough said!"
> —*Elyse*

Keep Your Bags Packed
Kimberlie, 10

We always had a bag packed so we wouldn't have to scramble in the middle of the night if I got a fever and we had to rush to the hospital. My mom bought doubles of every kind of food I liked, and we had a crate packed with many different things.

The Biggest Room, and the Farthest Away
Sarah, 11

Always try to get the biggest room you can. If you have a bigger room, you can bring in more stuff. Also, we tried to get as far away as we could from the nurses' desk, because at night it was really noisy.

    We had moving in down to a science. We got a transport chair that's like a wheelchair, but it's easier to collapse and put in the back of the car. We also had a cooler with wheels that we'd bring. I'd bring my own pajamas, all different kinds of pajamas. I was known for my pajamas. Comfy pajamas are a good present for people to give kids in the hospital. We had things packed all the time, because if I got a fever, it was back to the hospital immediately. We had to be ready to go.

Okay, Tell Us About the Catheter
Mason, 16

I woke up from the surgery on my leg and didn't know that I would have a catheter inserted. It freaked me out more than anything. Waking up and finding something sticking out of your body is a big deal, especially if you don't know it's going to be there. No one thought to tell me about that. I just woke up and there it was! I guess the doctors put catheters in so often they just don't think about telling the patient. Sometimes doctors leave out those little details!

> **cath-e-ter:** medical tube inserted into the body to remove fluids, especially after surgery when the patient can't get up to go to the bathroom

Pizza Delivery
Kimberlie, 10

You can order pizza in the hospital, and get it delivered. Don't ever forget that option.

Starbright World
Autumn, 11

See if your hospital has Starbright World. You can talk to other kids in other hospitals. It was like a video camera that they have, so other kids can see and hear you, and you can see and hear them. It really made a difference to me to talk to other kids in the hospital.

Stop the Hospital Food at the Menu
Hope, 12

Whatever you do, don't even let them bring the food trays into your room. They'll just gross you out and make you sick. Don't even ask what's on the menu! Also, don't eat food in there that you normally love because you'll probably throw it up. Once you throw it up, then you never want it again. It ruins you for life.

No Pop-In Visits
Mason, 16

Surprise visits are never recommended. Don't do the "pop-in" thing. It's all about the patient at all times—not about anyone or anything else. People mean well, and I understand that, but nothing matters but the patient and his recovery. If we're up to it, we really want to see people, anything to take our minds off being in there. But if we are not up to it, visitors, even with the best of intentions, can be a burden.

When people visit they feel like they have to be talking constantly. My mom and dad would sit for hours with me and say nothing. They knew what I needed, and they always focused on me without being overbearing. My friends always made me feel good in the hospital because they'd come in laughing and having fun, not sorrowful like older relatives.

Friends, more than family, are usually good about calling. They'd call and say, "Can I visit you?" I'd say, "Maybe not right now, thanks." They could ask a hundred times and be all right about rejection. The parent and the patient's advocates should be the line between their kid and visitors. It's okay if someone gets mad for being told this is not a good time to visit. My mom may have become unpopular with some of our family members because her best and only interest was my well-being and health. Her only goal when I was in the hospital was to take care of me. If that meant having visitors to take my mind off things, then that's what she allowed. If having visitors, no matter who they were, was not going to be good for me at that moment, she would not allow them to come.

If You Want to Visit, Make Sure You're Healthy
Mason, 16

If people are sick, even a little bit with only a cold, there is no way they should visit. Chemo really kicks your immune system in the butt. My mom would never let little kids visit because they're almost always sick with something. Also, nobody enters my room unless they wash their hands first. It was so annoying having all my friends constantly washing their hands, but I knew they had to. My mom's not a hovering mom, but now she's definitely protective of me in the hospital, and for all the right reasons.

How to Get Quicker Room Service
Hope, 12

When you're in the hospital for a while, the nurses might quit answering your buzzer or take forever to get back to you. If your parents aren't there to help you, pretend you're the parent asking for something. Ring your buzzer and use the deepest voice you can. Believe me, it really works! You get what you want a whole lot quicker! Even if you get caught, what are they gonna do, kick you out of the hospital?

I'm the Expert on Long Hospital Stays
Justin, 12

My advice is to try not to think about being in the hospital. Think about happy things; watch a movie or play a game. Bring posters, CDs, movies, and a notebook for drawing or writing. Sometimes I'd dabble in art. I have three journals from all my hospital stays. Write down a list of your favorite foods so, if anyone asks, you have a list because you can't always think of everything on the spot. Also, you definitely need to bring your own flashlight or nightlight. I used it mostly for reading. The hospital lights are obnoxious, either very bright or really dark. It's nice to have a little nightlight. Train your nurses to use flashlights at night instead of turning on the overhead lights. Take pictures of people, like nurses and friends. Put them in a scrapbook and write their names under the pictures, so you can remember them. Also, bring money—you can send your parents out to buy stuff for you, if you trust them. I trust my parents, somewhat. My mom always wrote me IOUs and paid me back.

They Really Are There to Help
Kimberlie, 10

The hospital can be a very dreadful place, but the doctors and nurses are there to help you get better. They are really nice, and are some of the best people I have ever known. They make you laugh when you are grumpy. They hug you when you are sad. They put stuffed animals on your bed when they know you have to be admitted to the hospital. They run down the hall to hug you when they see you.

Our hospital has a "Primary Card" so that, if you have nurses you particularly bond with, you can put them on your card so that when you get admitted your chances are greater of getting that nurse. They really work hard to get you the nurse on your card. It makes all the difference in the world.

Yucky Throw-Up Pans
Hope, 12

I have a really good idea, and that's to change the color of the throw-up pans. They're plastic and puke yellow. I think they need to make them pink or purple to make them more attractive. But the problem is that, after you throw up in pink or purple pans, then if you ever see pink or purple again, it will make you want to throw up all over again! Maybe they ought to draw a picture in the bottom of them, like a smiley face or of your crabby nurse.

The Sign on My Door
Mason, 16

EVERYONE PLEASE READ!

First of all, we all really do appreciate the love and support everyone is showing for us as a family and Mason as an individual.

SO, Please help us by . . .

NOT RINGING THE BELL.

NOT COMING UNANNOUNCED.

NOT BRINGING ANY SMELLY CHEESES, PERFUMES, AND/OR RELATIVES.

NOT GETTING (or not sharing if you DO get): PISSED, UPSET, UNLOVED, UNAPPRECIATED, UNINCLUDED, UNINVOVLED, UNSUPPORTIVE, UNSUPPORTED, JILTED, INCENSED, PUT-OFF, PUT-OUT, PUT UPON, OR _____ .

It is just better for Mason's healing to have it all happen on HIS time at HIS pace. It's for him. So ask, call ahead, and know we appreciate you all.

It Even Ruined Ice Cream for Me
Sarah, 11

One of the negatives of chemo is steroids. They make you take steroids to help your body accept the chemo. They do weird and painful things to your body. They made my bones ache and my face really puffy and fat. My friends would see me and say, "You look so different from last week." That's how fast it would happen.

I was two for my first round of chemo, and I couldn't swallow pills. My parents would crush up the prednisone pills and put it in food, like mostly ice cream. But it tasted horrible. It got to the point where I would say, "I don't want any more of *that* ice cream." Every time I'd eat ice cream, I'd be scared that white stuff would be in it, and I wouldn't eat it. We couldn't leave the hospital until I could take the prednisone three times a day. I always fought it. The hospital said that because I had trouble swallowing pills, they began teaching three-year-olds how to swallow pills.

Girl in My Bed . . . That's a Problem?
Mason, 16

I got into trouble one time because my girlfriend was in my hospital bed with me. You know how it is in the hospital room, there's one lousy little chair. She was first sitting on the bed and then just lay back with my stuffed monkey, Coco. My mom was outside in the hall. She was cool with it and even went out to give us some privacy. Sometimes you just need to be alone with your friends. We weren't doing anything, just watching a movie. The door was open and one of the nurses walked by. She told nurse Barri that I had a girl in my bed. Nurse Barri is really stern and never jokes around. She came in and yelled at me.

What made it worse was that my girlfriend was a volunteer at the hospital. She had been a Candy Striper for three years. She didn't want to lose her job. Nurse Barri came in and said it was "inappropriate." She yelled at my girlfriend, who was already scared of her. The girl felt absolutely horrible. My mom went to Barri and said, "Please don't get the girl in trouble. She's really a nice girl. They were just watching TV. She'd be really mortified if her mother found out that there was trouble." Nurse Barri was not willing to let it go so easily. She wasn't budging. But my mom finally talked her into letting it go, so no one got into trouble.

Un-Hospitable Therapy
Elyse, 13

Therapy has become my cuss word. Therapists are always the enemy. I called physical therapy (PT) "pain therapy" and "pain and torture." They would use all kinds of tricks to get you to do things. They'd say, "You'll get five stickers if you go on your tummy. Five stickers! That's a lot, Elyse." Yeah, right, five whole stickers. They wanted to get me to use my motor skills and move my hands and fingers and walk.

When I came out of the coma, they thought I had to be retaught *everything*—they didn't really know that I had not forgotten everything, like how to eat. During therapy, I'd go home on the weekends and eat regular food, like cheeseburgers. Then I'd come back on Sunday nights, and they'd give me pureed applesauce. They want to wean you back. I'd tell them, "I'm way past that! I'm eating cheeseburgers." But they have their regimen.

I also hated the parallel bars. They made me do them a million times, where you walk between the parallel bars. I wasn't really having difficulty walking. I just couldn't turn around at the end. That was the worst part. I got stickers for turning around! They kept them in a book. If you filled up your sheet, you got a prize, like stuffed animals. Then they kept making me do harder things. I'm thinking, what's the point of learning how to do these things if you are just going to give me harder stuff to do?

They tried to teach me how to use a wheelchair, but I wouldn't let them. I didn't want to learn how to use the wheelchair because I never wanted to be in a wheelchair. I tried to run over my physical therapist with my wheelchair, but I was too slow.

It Hurt to Look in the Mirror
Charon, 18

During chemo I lost a lot of weight. When I had my leg, I weighed 160 pounds. When they took it off, I weighed 98 pounds. I looked terrible. Before surgery, I'd look in the mirror and see nothing but muscles. After surgery, it just hurt to look in the mirror.

The Good
Autumn, 11

All of my Child Life people and most of my nurses were wonderful. They took extremely good care of me and made us kids feel like part of a family. When I came in for my visits, they would actually fight over who was going to get me. My favorite nurse left to be a travel nurse. When I relapsed, she came back just to take care of me. She would pull me around in a wagon through the halls at midnight. She'd take me downstairs and gave me anything I wanted.

Trying to Avoid Doing My Time
Mason, 16

I hated the hospital so much I would drink cold water to throw off my temperature. Once, I stuck the thermometer under a lamp so it made my temperature 108, but my mom knew something was up. She was always on to me.

The "Adult" on the Kids' Floor
Luke, 22

I played jokes on the nurses. They had the foam hand cleaner when you first walk in the room. I pulled it out and had it in my bed to spray them when they walked in. They would halfway expect me to do something. They'd come to my room and I'm not there because I'd go for walks around the hospital. I didn't actually leave the hospital, but I'd walk around it.

Even though I'm not a child anymore, they let me stay on the children's floor because I know all the nurses and everybody. I was usually the oldest patient on the floor. Being 22, I felt a little silly being on the children's floor, but I'd still press for it. They just treat you better on the children's floor. They're a lot more fun-loving. On the adult floor, they're old and mean and not cute.

I didn't actually hate the hospital. I didn't like missing out on things while being in the hospital. A couple of my friends got married and I wasn't able to go to the weddings because I was in the hospital. Once, I talked the doctor into writing me a note so I could go out with my friends for the night.

Cashin' In
Justin, 12

If you have cancer, you can milk it to make money in the hospital. I learned how to make beaded lizards and sold them at the hospital. I made some big dollars off of it. I sold lizards for one to four dollars. A lot of the nurses and doctors bought quite a few of them. I had a sign on my door, "Lizards for Sale."

I Grew Up in the Hospital—Those Are My People!
Catyche, 20

I don't remember a time when I wasn't going in and out of the hospital. I thought it was normal for kids to constantly go to the hospital. My best friends were doctors and nurses. That was hard because when I'd go back to school, I felt so different. I felt like they weren't my friends. I felt most like myself in the hospital because I grew up there.

Urine Sample

Charon, 18

In the hospital, I met Matthew. He was 10 and told me what he did to his nurse. You have the little cups that you put your urine in. He put apple juice in his cup and set it on the counter. When the nurse came in, he grabbed the cup and asked, "Do you need this?" The nurse said, "Yes." He drank it! He said the nurse about fainted.

Big Tumors, Little Miracles

Autumn, 11

When I was five, the doctor told my parents that the cancer cells had outgrown my blood supply, which meant that they had to open me up. The surgeon told my mom, "There is no way that we are going to be able to get the main tumor. It's just mangled in vessels, tissues, and organs, and I'd do more harm than good to your daughter to try and get it out. I'll take out whatever I can, but I can't get it all." My mom told him, "You do whatever you have to do because there is only one person who can save her, and if it's God's will to do it through your hands, so be it." The doctor said, "It's not like he's going to reach down here and take the tumor out."

My surgery took five hours. The doctor said that after he opened me up, he couldn't find my gall bladder or pancreas because I had this huge tumor that covered the whole right side of my body. All of my organs were squeezed on the left side. I had another huge tumor in front of all of my organs and my ovary was way bigger than it should have been. All of my insides were covered with cancer so that if you stretched out my intestines I wouldn't have had half an inch that didn't have cancer on it.

After the surgery, the doctor went out to my parents and said, "You better put a smile on your face because that tumor was just laying in there unattached, waiting on someone to pick it up and take it out." My mom said, "Not like God reached down here and took it out, but he sure untangled that mess so you could, didn't he?"

My First Words

Elyse, 13

I woke up from the coma after two and a half months and went home for a visit. Going home really helped me become more awake. I went back to the hospital and the next day, Dr. Sri, who isn't my regular doctor, came into the room without knowing I was out of the coma. It was near Valentine's Day, and he said, "Hi, Elyse, did your boyfriend get you these balloons?" I said, "I don't have a boyfriend." He about fell over. We all started laughing. He said, trying to recover, "Well, when are you going to get a boyfriend?" I said, "You'd better ask my dad."

Kicking the Habit
Mason, 16

I was really good about weaning myself off pain medication and narcotics. I really made an effort at that. I was good about feeling pain and knowing what the levels were, what I needed, and when I needed it. I didn't want to take anything that I didn't need to take.

But one time they did take me off my pain meds too soon. It was a day or two after my knee surgery. I was on a hardcore pain reliever eight times stronger than morphine. They took away the pump that self-regulates the medicine. The pump is set at a certain rate and, no matter how much you pump it, it only administers every six minutes. I think it's partly psychological that if you're pumping it, you're getting the pain meds. When they tried to move me from my bed, I almost passed out. Everything went white. It was the worst pain ever. I guess they try to get you off pain meds as soon as possible. I wasn't ready for the transition. I think I have a high threshold for pain, but this pain put me under.

There was another time—of course, it always happens in the middle of the night when there are no doctors around. My mom was there and ended up chasing down the nurses in the hallway saying, "You've got to give him something right now! I've never heard him in so much pain, and he's really screaming."

When those things happen, if you don't have anybody there, it's hard to get the doctors on the phone. You're desperate. There were a few of those moments. They never taught me to control the pain without drugs, which I think would be a good thing.

Shaving My Doctor's Head
Kimberlie, 10

I got to shave my doctor's head. It was fun—the ultimate revenge. They call St. Patrick's Day "St. Baldrick's Day." If you raise enough money—the money is for kids' cancer research—one of the doctors will shave their head, and a bunch of the nurses, too.

Dr. Olsen said that she would shave her head if we raised $25,000. She didn't think we could do it, but everyone really wanted to see her bald. On St. Baldrick's Day, we got to shave her head. Some of the nurses colored their hair with food dye really crazy colors because they knew they were going to shave it off. One of the nurses wanted to do it, but her fiancé wouldn't let her because they were getting married in a week. We let her off the hook!

How I Know When I'm Really Sick
Catyche, 20

When you're a normal kid and you get sick, *everyone* brings you balloons. But if you always get sick, and you're in and out of the hospital, then your extended family gets sick of visiting you, and giving you balloons and stuff. I don't get visitors or stuff too often unless I get *really* sick. Last fall, I got a whole bunch of balloons, so I knew I was pretty sick.

Syringe Wars
Justin, 12

We used to have "syringe wars" with these really big syringes. We'd fill them with water and squirt them. I'd ride around on my IV pole, with someone pushing me, looking for someone to squirt. I also had this water gun, and one nurse suggested that I hide it under the blanket and then when another nurse came in to take it out and squirt her. He said, "Just don't squirt me. That's the deal." I didn't squirt him, but I squirted the other nurses. They never got mad. They took it all in fun.

Having Fun in the Hospital
Aaron, 15

Me and my friend Joyce (I'm telling on you now, girl!) were in the hospital this one time, and we thought this guy in there was really cute. He was a patient. We went to the front desk and started prank-calling this boy. It was so funny. He'd answer the phone and I'd say, "You are so cute," and hang up. He'd ask, "Who keeps calling?" Joyce said, "It's your future girlfriend," and hang up. I think he found out it was us, because he gave us this "look" once in the kitchen. I was such a wimp, I said, "I didn't do it. She did it." I ratted out Joyce.

Ya know what else we did? It would be, like, 7:00 at night, and I'd bring my radio out and turn the music on, and we'd model up and down the hallway. We'd do it with our IV poles. Our parents thought we were crazy! The nurses always enjoyed it.

Drug Addicts
Catyche, 20

Some hospital employees think that people with sickle cell are faking it just to get drugs. I'm not saying there aren't people like that, but you can't treat everybody like they're drug addicts. When I'm at home, I can control my own medication and I know how much I need. I know when I have pain and I can take medicine to help me. That's no problem. But when I'm in the hospital I can't bring my own medicine from home and take it when I need it. I'll ask for medicine when I have pain and they'll say, "You don't look like you have pain." They act like they know how I'm feeling. Or they'll go, "Oh fine! I guess I'll have to call the doctor again!" They'll say it like they're annoyed with me. It's hard to get across how much pain you're in and that you need medicine.

Moments of Bonding
Mason, 16

We used to have great conversations in the hospital—my mom, dad, and me. We'd stay up until, like, 2:00 a.m. and just talk. I've always been open with my parents. They've always known most of the stuff that I've done. Also, we got goofy a lot in the hospital. We laughed our heads off. We'd use humor a lot to try and lighten up the situation. I'd act like I did before I had cancer. I tried to make everyone feel like it was fine and there was nothing to worry about.

It's Like Losing Your Freedom
Aaron, 15

I think we all have our times when we get sad and depressed. After a while, you just get fed up with being in the hospital all the time, and having everything taken away from you. You really do lose your freedom. I'm in the hospital normally for four to six weeks, then they let me out for a week, and then they put me back in for six weeks. Only for two weeks in that four to six week time period can I leave my room. I can't leave even to go get water because my counts are so low and I can get sick.

The two weeks that I can leave my room, I have to wear a mask. I can't have too many visitors. My mom is the only one who can come see me. When I'm really sick I just want to lie in bed. Joyce (my friend I met in the hospital) and me can see each other, but we either both have to be neutropenic, or we both have to not be neutropenic, and neither one of us can have a fever. There are too many rules to remember.

> **neu·tro·pe·nic:** having a really low white blood cell count, which makes you more prone to having fevers or getting sick; can be a side effect of chemotherapy treatments

It really is like being a prisoner with no say-so over your own life. I hate other people making decisions about my life, even if it is for my own good.

Don't Fight What You Know You Have to Do
Hope, 12

I used to fight going to the hospital, because I hated the place more than any place I can think of. I kept dragging my feet and dragging my feet, not wanting to go to the hospital when I knew we had to go. I kept hiding the thermometer because I knew that if my fever got too high, I'd have to go. Once when I hid the thermometer, by the time my parents got me to the hospital, I had gone into septic shock and almost died. I won't ever fight it again.

Don't Be Bashful in the Hospital
Mason, 16

You need to tell the doctors and nurses honestly how you feel. If you're in a lot of pain, or feel sick, let the doctors know. Don't hold it back. They can't help you unless you are completely honest with them—and they won't get mad at you if you tell them you hurt.

How you pay attention or react to things is really important. I paid attention to doses, rates, and amounts of infusion. I knew everything that went into me and through me. I asked a lot of questions. I asked what medicine they were putting in the IV, and when and how often. I wanted to know what was happening to me. I wanted to be part of the process.

Pay attention and ask questions. This is very important because you may ask a question that triggers something. One night, a young resident came into my room and started to give me something that I had a bad reaction to before. I called him on it because I knew that they were supposed to be giving me something else. If I hadn't, it would have been really bad for me.

Noise Factor
Aaron, 15

One of the biggest problems is that the nurses never close our doors. We had to make signs time and time again on our doors that read: "Please, shut the door." It didn't really bother us too much during the day when they'd leave the door open, but at night, you'd be sleeping and the nurses come and give you medicine, and they'd leave your door wide open. The noise is just horrible. You hear the nurses talking and laughing. You hear people's buzzers going off. You hear IVs going off. There is absolutely no way to sleep with your door open. It's just impossible. Sometimes we'd even yell to them, "Shut up out there!"

I Was an IV Guru
Miriam, 19

My nurses had a great time with me because I was such an easy patient. I wouldn't call them if my IV started beeping. I'd fix it myself, although I wouldn't touch the IV if it was beeping for medicine or chemotherapy. If it was just for IV fluid or to flush me, I would set it myself, or if it had air bubbles, I would clear it myself. You learn so many things when you're in the hospital. That's why I *don't* want to become a doctor!

Is there a Doctor in the House?
Scotty, 11

One Sunday in the hospital, I was in lots of pain. They couldn't get a doctor to come and give me something for the pain. It's a hospital! Where else do you find doctors? On the golf course? It took two hours to get a doctor. I was in severe pain. My mom offered to take me to the ER so I could be treated. She was so annoyed.

Nurse Makeovers

Autumn, 11

Somebody had given me all this play makeup, and I would always put the makeup on the nurses. One time, one of the nurses forgot she had it on—round circles on her cheeks and glitter on her eyelids. She forgot her house key, so she had to go to the gym where her husband was. When she walked in her husband looked frantic.

Another nurse forgot she had my makeup on, and went home and looked in the mirror and scared herself. Most of them would bring me makeup, because they knew I liked doing makeovers. They lined up every day before they left and wanted me to make them up. I never charged them for the makeover, but I could have, and they would have paid.

Pinky Paid the Price

Mason, 16

My girlfriend actually dated someone else while I was undergoing chemo. All the nurses said, "You shouldn't be treated that way. Trash Pinky." Pinky was the stuffed animal my girlfriend had given me. So Pinky the unicorn had to pay the price.

Snowball Fights

Sarah, 11

There was a big snowstorm while I was in the hospital. I wanted to play in the snow, but I was stuck in my room and not allowed to go outside. My mom went outside, got a big bowl of snow, and brought it up to my room. I made snowballs and threw them at this old nurse. I thought she would get mad, but she handled it very nicely. It took guts to throw a snowball at her. Afterwards, I think she squirted me with a water syringe.

I'll Bet You've Never Heard of This Diet

Aaron, 15

Sometimes I would be on a neutropenic diet in the hospital, which means I couldn't eat food with bacteria (the food has to be really cooked), and I couldn't eat fresh vegetables and fresh fruit. For example, the skin on an apple has a lot of bacteria. The food has to be prepared a certain way—basically overcooked and well done. Then I have to eat it while it's really hot. I could only eat frozen food nuked in the microwave. If my food was cooked at home, it had to be immediately frozen, then nuked in the microwave at the hospital. My counts had gotten so low that any bacteria could really hurt me. I can't tell you how *not*-delicious that stuff was, and so hot you could hardly taste it.

Even My PJs Had to Be Sterilized
Autumn, 11

I had to be careful where I went for six months after my stem cell transplant because it had killed my immune system and made me susceptible to fever. When I went out, I had to wear a mask. I couldn't go to school the whole year. I couldn't even go to the mall, because there were too many people—too many germs. I did get to go to my friend's house, but everyone had to wear a mask. My friends didn't like wearing the masks. You can't breathe and you feel like you're suffocating. My mom had to sleep with one on when she would spend the night in my hospital room. For a while, everyone in my hospital room had to wear masks.

They let me wear my own pajamas, except mom had to wash them, dry them, put them in a plastic bag, and freeze them. This would make sure that all the germs were dead.

Sarah's Nail Salon
Sarah, 11

I started a nail salon in the hospital. I had a sign on the door of my hospital room reading: "Sarah's Nails." All the nurses came and got their nails painted. I charged them, and I was actually making money in there. My dad says it was to help pay all the medical bills.

I painted my dad's toenails in a rainbow, but I didn't make him pay. It was Easter and we were having a neighborhood Easter egg hunt. I told him that he had to wear his sandals during the Easter egg hunt with his rainbow nail polish on his toes so everybody could see it. He did it, even though he said that it was too cold outside to wear sandals.

Grandma, the Taste Tester
Jessica, 12

When they brought the food trays into my room, my mom and I would look at each other and say, "Do we dare?" My grandma will eat anything. She came for lunch one day and it looked like some sort of tuna casserole. I'm not sure what it was. She took a bite and even she didn't like it. If Grandma doesn't like it, there's something wrong with it.

Fake Poo-Poo
Autumn, 11

My friends came to the hospital a lot to visit me. One time was really funny. One of my friends' little brother brought me some rocks. I had just had surgery and everyone was waiting on me to go to the bathroom and do number two. They were just standing around, waiting for this big moment. The brown rocks were on my bed. Suddenly, someone yelled, "Look, she had a bowel movement!" It was so funny!

You Just Can't Get a Good Night's Sleep
Mason, 16

As much as I love small children, in the hospital I prefer a room away from them. There could be a child who was uncontrollable, crying and yelling all night. Some nights were horrible. Once, this kid was screaming nonstop at the top of his lungs all night long. I felt bad for the baby, but after a while you just don't want to hear it anymore. It's tough enough to sleep in the hospital, but when there is a kid crying all night, you might as well just give up trying.

Hospital Matchmaker
Autumn, 11

I helped set up a romance in the hospital. Todd was a volunteer, and there was a nurse named Rebecca. They got to liking each other very, very much. One day, Todd called Rebecca and said he had a birthday present for me. He called me afterward and said it was really an engagement ring for her, and that it was a surprise.

He put the ring in all these little and big boxes and told Rebecca to take it to work with her because it was my birthday present. Rebecca gave it to me and watched as I started unwrapping it and taking out the boxes. Todd was standing quietly behind Rebecca holding a rose. She didn't know he was there. I finally got to the last box. I opened it up the wrong way, then turned it around and opened it up again and said, "I want to know if you will marry Todd." It was a huge diamond. She was completely shocked, and she said, "Yes." They got married and I went to the wedding. It was beautiful.

Chapter 6

Family Fun and Fuss

"My whole family was devastated the night we found out that I relapsed. I told them, 'I beat it once, I'll beat it again.'" —Sarah

"My parents always tried to get me to focus on my abilities, and not my disability." —Jonathan

"I told my mom, 'If you got paid for worrying, we'd be living in a mansion.'" —Scotty

---

Our illnesses change everything in our families. Our parents, aunts, uncles, and grandparents worry about every little bump we get, if our wigs are on straight, if we do our daily therapy, and they go crazy if a fake eyeball falls out in public. Sometimes an illness brings us closer to our brothers and sisters because now we have more important things to worry about. But yeah, we still fight with them. Sometimes they're jealous of us—if you can believe that—because of the attention we get. And sometimes we keep our true feelings from our families, because they really have enough to deal with.

How Moms Are

Hope, 12

In the hospital, my parents always spend the night. When my mom stays the night, she'll ask me if I need something and I'll say, "No." She'll be like, "Are you sure?" That's what a mom does. When my dad would ask me if I needed anything, and I said no, he'd say, "Okay." My dad tells me that's just the difference between moms and dads.

> "My parents make me do chores even though I'm in a wheelchair. I'm not sure if I like that."
> —*Lindsey*

The Girl Who Cried Wolf

Catyche, 20

I played a lot of pranks on my mom. It sounds mean now, but it was really funny at the time. It was right after they finally let me go home after I woke up from my coma. The funniest thing I ever did was pretend to pass out in the backyard. I had my sister yell for mom. When she rushed outside, she saw me on the ground spread-eagle. Mom panicked. Another time, I pretended to have a seizure just to trick her. Now she doesn't pay attention to me. It would be funny if I really did get sick. It will be like the girl who cried wolf.

My Brother Is Jealous

Mookie, 12

I've gotten extra attention since we found out I have Hodgkin's disease. Almost every week, I get a new toy or a new pair of sneakers. My brother gets jealous. Sometimes we fight because he hates that I get a lot of stuff and he doesn't. He hates that I get homeschooled for an hour, and he has to go to school and stay there all day. He says that he's gonna break his arms and legs so he can stay home.

Sometimes my parents get upset about my cancer. My dad says he wishes he could take my illness from me so that I don't have to have it. Sometimes he gets sad and he'll cry. I tell him to not cry because everything's going to be okay. I try not to get upset in front of my parents.

I Try to Be Like My Daddy

Charon, 18

The person I always look up to is my daddy. He didn't let anything hold him down. I wasn't gonna let anything hold me down. He never showed any type of pain. I'm picking all of that up from him. That's what helped me get through all the things I've been through, and am still going through. I think about how he'd take it and that's how I take it.

The Day I Found Out That Camp Was ONLY a Mile Away

Cassidy, 7

I go to a camp every summer for regular kids, which is cool to me since I'm blind. I go for five nights, and I go swimming, play basketball, and do cheerleading. I always thought camp was a long way away because we'd get in the car and drive forever. Then one day, my mom let it slip that camp was only a mile away, but my parents drove me around in the car for hours so it felt like I was going a long way away to camp. I was so mad. I think they wanted me to think camp was far away 'cause then I'd think it was cooler. That's a disadvantage to being blind—your parents can make you think things are far away when they're right down the street.

My Brother Mentors Me

Justin, 6

It feels good knowing my older brother has hemophilia and a port, too. He helps me because he knows things. I'm learning about vein access, and not always going in through the port for my infusions. I'm a little nervous about doing it through the vein, but my brother says it is a lot quicker and doesn't hurt. If my big brother can do it, then I can do it, too.

Hoping It's the Last Time
Luke, 22

I have four sisters—one younger and three older. My younger sister was the only one who was at home since I've been sick, and we're a lot closer. She's two years younger than I am and we've always been close. I think it's really hard on her. She's scared, which I can understand. If she were sick, I would be devastated. She doesn't talk to me much about it. I think she might be in denial. She would just rather not think about it. She asks me how I'm feeling, but everybody does that and they all get the same answer: "I'm great!" I say that all the time, even if I'm not feeling great.

My parents worry about me a lot. Mom's better at handling it than Dad is. He worries, but won't talk about it. I know it really bothers them, but there's nothing they can do. It gets harder for them every time I go into the hospital. They're always hoping this will be the last time. Then it's not.

We Still Argue Like Brothers
Matthew, 9

My brother and I, even though we both have hemophilia, still argue like brothers. We have separate rooms, and we fight about going into each other's room. We fight about who has the coolest port. But what's cool is that we can talk about things without having to ask each other 50 questions. Also, my brother is the one I admire the most. He's always there for me.

My Little Brother Is Having Trouble Coping
Elyse, 13

As mad as I get about my injuries, I think it makes my little brother even more mad, and embarrassed. He says, "Elyse, don't go in your wheelchair, people look at you like you're weird." I tell him, "So what if they think I'm weird. I am weird, you're weird, Mom's weird."

My Sister Gets Jealous—If She Only Knew

Sarah, 11

People are bringing me gifts all the time. Ask my sister if she thinks that's fair, and she'll tell you "No!" It seems to her like I get so much extra, but I would give up all the presents just to be normal. My sister just doesn't get it. We share a room, and like most sisters we fight about clothes and space. You know, the typical stuff. Before cancer, it seemed like I'd get yelled at no matter who started the fight. That's my side anyway. Sometimes I hit my sister and say, "Mom, Rachel hit me!" Since my cancer, Rachel gets blamed no matter what. Maybe that's a little unfair, but it's too much fun to stop.

My Sister Is Finally Starting to Understand

Abbie, 13

I don't fight with my older brother and younger sister as much as I used to. With my brother, my relationship is probably better because we used to fight all the time. Now we're closer and get along better. Both my brother and sister got jealous of me because of all the special attention I received (although my brother wouldn't admit it). He got mad and yelled at my mom, "Abbie, Abbie, Abbie! It's always about Abbie!"

My sister really struggled to understand what was going on with me. My mom explained to her that I had an illness. I don't know if she called it cancer. Mom told her exactly what was happening, and what was going to happen over the next year, that it would mean a lot of hospital and doctor visits. I think my sister is starting to understand things. It doesn't bother her anymore that her friends walk in and I don't have my wig on. Except one time when she was having a slumber party. I went down there with a flashlight and no wig and scared them; I was flipping the flashlight on and off. She didn't like that.

In the beginning, I think it bothered my sister to even look at me. I think she was also afraid that she might end up getting the same thing. Lately, she has come out of her shell and is loud and funny and obnoxious. I think it's to get the attention that she feels she wasn't getting. Now she uses me. She'll say, "Abbie, tell dad you want a pizza. He'll do anything for you." My brother uses me too. He told me to wish for a car from Make-A-Wish, even though I am only 13.

When I feel bad or hurt, I try to hide it from my parents because my mom gets so upset. I usually go into my room and shut the door to hide it from her. I eventually talk to her. My mom and I have gotten closer with us both home together all the time. My dad says we're "two peas in a pod." We even argue less than before I had cancer. It is going to be interesting this fall when I go back to school. I think it will be hard for both of us—separation anxiety.

We Had a Plan
Autumn, 11

When I got sick, my parents had to decide who would quit their job to take care of me. My dad worked for the Department of Defense and had insurance. My mom worked for a tire company and also did computer consulting. She didn't have any benefits, so she stayed home with me. My parents work very well together as a team. My mom spends nights with me in the hospital, and my dad gets my siblings off to school each morning. Every other day, Dad comes to the hospital to let Mom spend time with my siblings. If I'm in the hospital over the weekend, Dad takes the weekend shift at the hospital, unless he has National Guard duty. The Guard would give dad the weekend off if he needed it. We've been very blessed. When I had surgery, I wouldn't allow anyone but my dad to move me, including the nurses. So the 16 days after surgery, he had to be here. He knew how to pick me up and not hurt me.

Laughter Is the Best Medicine
Kimberlie, 10

I did a trick on my mom that she still has gray hair from. We were getting ready to go to bed and my muscles were really sore. We have this tube-like thing that you heat it in the microwave and put on your muscles to help relax them. It was like four days after I got diagnosed. My mom went out of the room for a second, and I put the heated tube on my forehead. When my mom came back in, I took it off and I said, "Mom, I feel hot." Fevers are a very bad thing when you have leukemia. They can be very dangerous. She felt my head and she goes, "Oh, my God, you're burning up!" She was going to call the hospital. Sometimes the best medicine is laughter.

My Brother Still Tortures Me

Justin, 12

I have a brother, Ben, who is 15. Do we get along? Not a chance. Does he wait on me when I'm sick? Not a chance. We fight a lot, not physically but verbally. We fight about everything you can think of (it's a long list). When he gets in trouble, he always blames it all on me. He gets mad when I wrinkle up his favorite book when I'm reading it. He gets mad about the way I chew my food, but he doesn't do any better. That's what brothers are for, I guess—to torture you.

Better Ways to Bond

Mason, 16

My dad had prostate cancer. He was diagnosed in December and in January had surgery. My parents timed it so I wasn't having chemo during that time, so we could all be with my dad in the hospital for those days. He didn't make a big deal out of it at all. He played it down. Compared to what I had, it didn't even seem like cancer. I wasn't worried because he had the greatest attitude, no worries. He just had the surgery, and that was it. He didn't have chemo or anything. My uncle also had prostate cancer a couple of months before that. We didn't bond over cancer. There are better things to bond over.

Just Don't Touch My Stuff

Charon, 18

I didn't want to tell my brothers and sister about my cancer. I don't remember telling them anything. I think my mom told them. There are eight of us, I'm number six. Six of us still live at home. They're not different toward me now that I have cancer. We still fight the same and all. I mostly argue with my one brother. He wants all the stuff I get from being sick. I don't like for anyone to touch my stuff without asking me. He's like, "But you get all this stuff!" I say, "Yeah, but I don't ask for it. I just get it." We don't argue about anything else except him touching my stuff. I don't share my room with anybody. I mostly stay in my room and do my homework. Since my dad died, a whole lot of things changed. I really can't explain it. Things just aren't how they used to be. My mom has to work all the time, and there's a lot of stuff that needs to be done around here. I try to do all I can to help, with one leg.

I Hate Physical Therapy—But I Can't Give It Up
Blayne, 19

I hated, and still hate, physical therapy. It hurts. It's hard. When I was 14, my mom said, "You don't have to go anymore. You don't have to wear your leg braces anymore. You don't have to do anything anymore." I jumped at it! I was like, "Yes, my mom doesn't care! Cool!" I spent a year not doing anything, not even going to a doctor.

But then my own guilt was saying, "You know, this can't be good for me." I said to myself on my 15th birthday, "I know that I'm gonna ruin everything I've worked for my whole life." I called my doctor and booked an appointment. My mom came in and signed all responsibility over to me. Basically, in the eyes of the hospital, I was an adult. My mom didn't want to be involved. That was hurtful. She came for the first therapy session to give them all of my background stuff. She never came again.

Twice a week for five years now, through thick and thin, I've been going to physical therapy by myself. I did what I had to do. I booked all my doctors' appointments myself and used public transportation to get there. It was my decision, even though I hated it. I knew I needed it, even if my parents didn't support me.

Our Family Has Gotten Closer
Kimberlie, 10

I am very lucky because my family always shows me how much they care about me by how well they take care of me. I know all the fuss is for my own good, even though sometimes it's hard. My family is always there for me whenever I need them, whether it is to have a shoulder to cry on, someone to tell a joke to, or someone to hug. My big sister has been a great big sister. I think it has been very hard on my sister for all kinds of reasons, but she has also been understanding. I think my sister and I are closer than before because we know what is really important, and fighting isn't worth it. I think our family has gotten closer because we spend even more time with each other.

My Brother Was Always There
Mason, 16

My brother Toby was really scared when we found out about my cancer. He had just turned 13, and we have always had a good relationship. The cancer really didn't change much, which I'm glad about. I knew that it totally affected him. We'd still fight—after all, we're brothers—but we also have a lot of fun together. I think we got a lot closer through it all.

When we found out about my cancer, Toby was at a skateboarding camp in Pennsylvania. When he got back, I wanted to be the one to tell him because of the relationship we have. I said, "I have cancer." I just blurted it right out. He said, "Don't say that." I think he didn't really know what to say or what to think. I said, "I'm not kidding you." He asked if I was going to die. Dad said, "We're all gonna go at some point, but we're going to get Mason's health back so he's really old when he goes."

It was just unreal for him. When I showed Toby my Hickman port in my chest, it became more real for him. He wanted to hear things from the doctors, so he came to a few of the meetings we had with the doctors and asked a lot of questions. The doctors were really good about addressing Toby's questions. He knew what cancer was, but he didn't know how serious it was. He mostly wanted to know if I was going to die. The doctor said, "He'll be fine." It was good that he was able to hear that from the doctor.

One of my parents was always in the hospital with me. Toby never got jealous of that. I think he knew that I needed that. Our parents always tried to be there with me, and also home with Toby. They made sure I was never alone. But still, it must have been hard on Toby. He looked at it really positively. I know it made Toby stronger, more self-reliant. Toby visited me in the hospital a couple of times a week after school. He came on his own. My parents never had to guilt him into visiting. That made a big difference to me. That's a big deal because hospitals are weird places, especially for kids. He came to visit a lot, but I don't think he ever got used to it. What was good about Toby visiting was that the moment he came through the door, he was exactly who he had always been—silly and goofy. He'd do goofy things on purpose. We always joked around. I know he was trying to cheer me up and keep me laughing, like we do at home. It helped to keep things as they always were.

I'll Never Be "Fixed"—and That's Okay

Blayne, 19

My little sister made a really strange connection. About a year ago, I had to be in a cast for corrective issues at the same time that my brother, Josh, broke his arm and had to be in a cast. We had always told my sister from the time she was really little that my legs were "broken." Not in the sense that the bones were literally broken, but in the sense that my legs just didn't work right. She logged that in the back of her brain, and never asked any questions. Then Josh got his cast off, and he was fine. Obviously, I'm not going to come out of the cast and everything's gonna be fine. But she thought that I should be fine, like Josh.

My sister came with me when I got my cast off. Her response was, "Okay, get up and walk." I'm like, "What are you talking about?" She said, "Your legs were broken, you got them in a cast, now you can walk!" I had to just break her heart and say, "My legs are never going to be fixed. They can get better, but they're not ever going to be fixed. And you know what? That's okay. That's fine because that's what makes me who I am. You have brown hair. I have brown hair. You have legs that work; mine don't." She has become one of the most accepting people I know.

> "You gotta try and find the positive in everything. You can't dwell on the negative." —Aaron

I've always been so open about it, and I've told her everything that she wants to know. The very first time we ever saw someone who walked like me in a store, she walked up to the guy and said, "You walk like my brother." He was surprised. I walked up and we sat in the food court talking. It was amazing. My sister had never made the connection that there are other people out there who have disabilities. Because she doesn't view it as a disability—Blayne's legs just don't work right, that's all.

Nurse Daddy
Amber, 15

While my mama was at work all day, daddy took care of me. I would be too weak to take a shower by myself, so daddy had to help me. I wasn't embarrassed or nothing because you have to do what you have to do when you're in a situation like this. I was grateful that my daddy was there to help me shower. Also, I'd be too weak to be able to make it to the bathroom in time. I had to wear diapers in case of an accident. It's okay if you have to do that. You gotta do what you gotta do to survive this cancer. Don't be ashamed.

Mitey Grandparents
Mason, 16

My grandparents on my dad's side have this horse farm called "Misty Meadows." Grandmolly has always loved horses, and Grandpa started this therapeutic riding program for handicapped children called the "Mitey Riders." I really admire what he does with these kids. He's great! I help out with the program when I have time.

Miracles Can Happen
Amber, 15

I get along better with my siblings now since I got cancer, especially my brother. Every chance he gets he says, "Amber can I do this, or that, for you?" I'll want something to drink and he'll say, "I'll get it for you." That didn't happen before. Christy, my sister, will put a blanket on me if I'm lying on the couch. She tends to me now. I used to tend to her before my cancer. She's a miracle baby because, when she was born, she weighed two pounds and they said she wouldn't make it. Now she's 30 years old. We know miracles happen. The newspaper called and asked my mama what we were looking for, and she said, "A miracle."

Jealousy Will Get You Nowhere
Aaron, 15

I have one brother who lives with me and my mom. My brother is jealous because I get a lot of special treatment from everybody—people send me money and raise money for me and do a lot of different things. They'll send me cards, and I have boxes full of them. My brother doesn't get the attention that I get. I don't really understand what he's going through, but I wish I could. I can understand why he's jealous. He thinks that, no matter what I ask for, mom will give it to me. I, of course, have a different view. My mom will give me small things. Like when we're at the store and I want a new CD, I'll beg a little, and she'll get it for me. My brother won't get the CD even if he begs for it.

But I think we're treated different for another reason. I get good grades and he doesn't. When I come home from the hospital (because I have nothing else to do), I cook, I clean, I do laundry, and all that. So there's a difference in our behavior. Mom wouldn't treat us differently if he did what he was supposed to. So it's not because of my cancer—it's because of everything else.

He's sad that I have cancer though, and he tells me he worries about me. Yester-day, I was really tired, and I was upstairs in my room sleeping. He came to my door every half hour and asked, "Aaron, are you okay? Do you want me to get anything for you? Are you thirsty? Are you hungry?" That's when he gets a little sad.

Like an Old Married Couple
Miriam, 19

The only person who treated me differently was my mom. I'm her first born, and her only daughter. I have one brother, three years younger. Poor thing, he was left back in fourth grade because of my illness. It's my fault, because my parents couldn't devote time to him. He's not angry about it. He's the first person to say, "My sister was sick. I had to be there for her. I had to forget about myself so I could help her." He's my best friend.

He won't abandon me to go be with his friends. I slept in his room most of the summer because I don't have an air conditioner in my room. Even then we argued. I'd be like, "Why didn't you clean up your room?" He was like, "I didn't clean the room 'cause I didn't think it was necessary." Just that kind of arguing, like an old married couple who really love each other. We never *really* fought. My mom says, "I raised weird kids."

Not for Big Things
Marian, 16

I am the oldest. I have a younger sister and a younger brother. My sister, when I was first diagnosed, felt really neglected. My brother doesn't really understand arthritis because he's only in first grade. He knows I have it, but a lot of times he even forgets that I have it. My sister remembers when I was diagnosed. She didn't understand it then, but now she helps me volunteer at the Arthritis Foundation. She has become pretty supportive. Because I got so much attention, I didn't realize that my sister might be jealous. I think she was just upset and maybe wanted more attention. I'd get mad at her and say, "I don't want this. It's not my fault. I would rather be you than me."

My mom is really strict and watches over me a lot. She's a lot more lax with my sister and lets her do more stuff than me. That's my take anyway. I'm pretty honest with my pain to my mother. But if I tell her I feel bad, I never get to go anywhere. So I tell her I feel fine. The next day, I feel horrible that I've done that. But I still do it. Sometimes I use my illness to get out of doing things, like taking out the trash, but never for big things.

My Family and My Fighting Fish
Faith, 20

I've lost both of my parents. My mom died of AIDS when I was 12. My dad was murdered. He was a security guard. He was getting off of work when two boys were arguing over drugs and one of them pulled out a gun and accidentally shot my dad in the
head. They're in jail in New Jersey. I was 15 when he got shot. I was close to my dad
and used to see him a lot.

I have a fish. He's a fighter, like me. It's a beta fish, a fighting fish. You can only
have one fish in the tank, because if you add another fish, he will kill it and eat it. My
niece brought over a goldfish. She put it in the tank, and the goldfish was real scared.
He was trying to get out, but he had nowhere to go. For some reason, the beta fish
didn't eat him.

Cancer Is a Family Affair
Aaron, 15

My cancer wasn't just a change in my life; it was a change for a lot of people. My
mom's life changed dramatically. She doesn't go out any more. She can't quit working
because she needs the money. That's what's so difficult. They work her 12 hours a day
and don't cut her any slack at all. If she leaves work early, she needs to make it up. It's
really hard for her. When I'm in the hospital, she doesn't sleep at night. She has to go
home because of my brother, but she can't sleep. If I call at 1:00 in the morning, she'll
pick up on the first ring.

Back to Nature
Blayne, 19

I attribute my acceptance of my disability to my dad and stepmom because when the
doctors were saying, "It would be a lot easier if you put him in a wheelchair," they said,
"No, this kid's going to walk." I did, but it was hard. I make a joke that I didn't know I
was handicapped until I was 14 because my parents never treated me differently.

I grew up in the middle of the Hoh Rainforest on the Olympic Peninsula in
Washington, basically in the middle of the woods. My father had grown up without
electricity, and he had this idea that bringing up five kids in the middle of the woods
without electricity or running water would be great for us. I'm not sure what possessed

him to do that. I think he felt that we would learn morals and values and how to survive.

We really did learn a lot. You really don't need electricity. We never had to camp 'cause we lived camping. We did nature things. I grew up using only kerosene lamps for light. We had a generator, but we only used it once a week to watch a movie. We had running water that came from a stream, so it wasn't safe to drink. But it did come into our bathroom and into our toilet. To take a bath, we would fill these big containers of water and carry them to the stove, heat them on the stove, pour the boiling water into the bathtub, turn on the cold water, and make it warm. It was a tough existence.

Reading is one of my favorite things to do. But my father thought reading was a waste of time and there were better things to do. I would sneak books and read them with a kerosene lamp. I discovered that if I put the book on one side of the lamp and me on the other side, and looked through the glass, I could read. I felt like Abraham Lincoln. My eyesight from doing that for five years isn't the greatest, but I read a lot of books that way.

No Excuses
Brittney, 15

My mom always tells us, "I know that you're sick, and I know that you guys have had a rough life, but that's no excuse to be disrespectful or mean to people. You're still going to have consequences. You're going to have a normal life like other kids." She always tries to help us look at the bright side of things. When we get down she'll say, "We've gotten a trip to Florida and a trip to Hawaii, we've gotten a pool, and we've got people in our community who have brought us gifts for Christmas, helped us through stuff, and donated money and had parties. We've had a lot of really wonderful things come to our family." But it's still incredibly hard. Having cancer is expensive. My dad works three jobs to pay the bills. Last year, he took off from two of the jobs because he wanted to spend time with all of us together because I was doing so well.

Using My Illness
Javlyn, 16

I have one brother. He's seven. We get along all right, but we fight. I don't think he treats me any differently because of my illness, except maybe he's sweeter. We might argue but he'll call me in the hospital and say, "When are you coming home?" When he was in kindergarten, his teacher said she could tell when I was sick because he talked so much when I was home, but very little when I was in the hospital. His teacher would ask him, "What's wrong?" He'd say, "I miss my sister." Then he started using it to his advantage. He'd say, "My sister's in the hospital and I don't feel good. Can I put my head down?" He's using my illness to get out of things in class!

Running Down My Family
Tonya, 20

I've run down my mama plenty of times with my wheelchair. I don't do it on purpose. My wheelchair is motorized and it's pretty heavy, and sometimes it slips away from me. Once, I did run over my brother on purpose. He was on the ground and let me do it. I was four, and he was 13. I'd run over him and just laugh. I thought it was the funniest thing in the world. We were just having fun, but it scared Mama to death.

Bowling for Blayne
Blayne, 19

We had this game called "Bowling for Blayne." You have to understand my family dynamics and how I was not pitied for being "disabled." I'd go walking through the yard, and I'd be tipping and turning because it isn't exactly a flat yard. My family, trying not to treat me as disabled, would pick up a ball and roll it at me, like bowling. It was all in fun, and they never really tripped me up. The truth was that I'd be laughing so hard by the time the game was over, I'd be on the ground myself. We had a blast with it.

The point is—it all depends on how you take the situation and how you examine it. I've been angry, been sad, been mad, and I've blamed it on my mom and dad: "You could have taken me here, you could have given me this surgery, and you could've done this and that . . . ."

The truth is you have to go through the "couldas" and the "wouldas" and the "shouldas." The bottom line is you're left with what you're left with, and you gotta work with it. We chose to have fun. My situation is what it is. I can't change the past, and my family never meant to do me wrong. It's just the way things are.

Chapter 7
Dealing with Our Public

"I really am a good person, but people just see me physically." —Tonya

"This book will get my word out. I want to help other kids." —Hope

"I've been through so much, nothing is going to seem hard anymore." —Elyse

Going out in public sometimes can be funny, frustrating, and embarrassing—or all three. Plus, whenever you put wheels under us, you know there are disasters lurking. You have people staring at you like you're from another planet and asking your parents what's wrong with you—right in front of you, like you can't speak. Sometimes they point or ask you stupid questions. But there are also the nice people who hold open doors or help us reach things. Here's what all that is like from our side. We'll give you our tips on how to get around better in public, if you're like us, or how to treat us in public, if you're not like us (basically, like other "normal" kids).

My Mom Won't Let Me Take My Eyes Out in Public
Cassidy, 7

I wear plastic eyes sometimes, since I don't have real eyes. In Sunday school class, we were acting up and the teacher said, "I want all eyes on me." I said, "My mommy said that I can't take my eyes out." Everyone laughed, except the teacher. Another time, this boy was sitting behind me in the movies kicking my chair. I turned around and said, "If you keep kicking my chair, my eyes are going to fall out." Then we were at an amusement park, standing in line to get on a ride. Suddenly my mom said, "Cassidy, push your eye back in again." I can't always feel when they fall out. People in line were just horrified and freaking out, I guess.

Scared Out of My Mind
Ryan, 18

My family and I all went to this big discount chain (you know which one I mean). We rushed through the door—me in my wheelchair—to go and look at the new toys and CDs. We got halfway through the door, and the greeter stopped us dead in our tracks. She started tugging on my arm saying, "You were in here just ten minutes ago. You were playing in those wheelchairs. That's store property. You need to get out of that wheelchair." Evidently, before we arrived, these other kids had been messing around in wheelchairs. When she saw us, she thought we were the same kids who came back to push her buttons. I don't look like I should be in a wheelchair—no distinguishing marks or visible signs that I can't stand up and walk away. It just looks like I'm sitting in the chair.

I was scared out of my mind thinking, oh my God, what do I do if this woman pulls me out of this chair? It's not like I could just stand up, walk away, and shrug it off. If she pulls me out of the chair, I'm on the floor in the middle of a store in public!

As this is running through my mind, my friend JC jumped in and said, "Lady, you need to let him go. I've known him my entire life and he hasn't walked once. It's his wheelchair, not the store's." But she kept saying sternly, "You need to get out of this chair now! This is store property!" I'm not saying anything. I'm shocked. She was an authority figure, and when you're 13 you're always feeling guilty about something. Your first thought is always, "What did I do now?" If I could have, I would have gotten up and ran off.

Then my parents come through the door. They saw this woman bent over me and pulling on my arm. My dad got angry and started yelling, "What are you doing?" Someone called security, so here comes two huge guys. They grab my dad and the woman still doesn't get it (and neither does security). The woman is still insisting that it's their wheelchair. Then my little sister gets scared and takes off. The situation escalates to the point where there are two big security guards holding my father back, and three more rushing toward me.

My dad is yelling, "You don't want to do this. Let go of my boy." I'm thinking that I'm going to be thrown onto the floor, have my hands zip-tied, and be restrained for something I haven't done. All because this woman is out of her mind.

My parents finally were able to get through to these people that I have cerebral palsy and the wheelchair was mine. The woman was shocked and started falling all over herself apologizing. The whole situation was just horrible, and then we were faced with finding my little sister. That was a whole other ordeal.

How People Try to Bond
Mason, 16

One interesting phenomenon that I've experienced is when I'm talking about my cancer, the first thing people usually say is, "My Aunt Edna had . . . " That's so commonplace, but I think they can't help it because it's human nature. I think it's some sort of weird way of trying to bond. Whether it's a disfigurement or cancer, people try to find that common ground to bond.

Great Icebreakers
Alan, 20

In public, people usually are very courteous to me. Sometimes people shout, like I can't hear. Or they'll talk really slowly. I have my response pre-programmed into my talking, portable computer: "I'm not deaf." A lot of times, people want to know about my equipment, especially the computer. Kids gravitate to my computer, but they stay a half step away because they're not sure. I'll smile at them or wave at them, and they'll come over. Children don't talk to me, but you can see that they're really interested in my computer.

Also, I wear a Metallica hat a lot. My computer and my Metallica hat are great icebreakers. So many people will ask, "Are you into Metallica? Me too!" Right off the bat, we start a conversation. When they see my computer, and that it can talk, it blows them away. It's an instant conversation starter.

What Really Puts Me over the Edge
Lindsey, 10

People ask my parents questions about me, right in front of me, instead of asking me! A salesperson will ask my mom, "Would she like a lollipop?" My mom will ask me, because she knows I hate it, "Lindsey, do you want a lollipop?" I say, "I really don't need a translator."

It also bothers me when they think I'm really stupid. Some people will look at me and actually say, "Look, she's MR (mentally retarded)." Then I'll say, "What did you just say? I'm physically challenged." It seems like everyone thinks that almost anybody in a wheelchair is mentally ill.

Sometimes kids will come up and say, "How'd you hurt your brain?" I say, "Who said anything was wrong with my brain?" They're like, "Oh, but you're in a wheelchair. I thought you had something wrong with your brain." So now one of my friends, every time I'm acting all funny and stuff, she's like, "Do you need your brain scanned again?"

It Just Makes Me Special
Justin, 6

If people ask me what my port is, I say, "It's a syringe that adds infusion." Then I explain what infusion is. It makes me feel special because I have something no one else has. Kids ask me about it at the beach, but I'm too busy having fun and just say, "That's my port, gotta catch that wave."

There's a Right Way and a Wrong Way
Charon, 18

After I got my leg amputated, my mama didn't want me to go anywhere. Maybe she thought I was gonna slow her down, or that someone would be rude to me. I started feeling better and started going out. I loved it! Going out in public is no big deal for me, even that first time. People are always gonna stare. There ain't nothin' I can do about it. Sometimes they glance at me then look away.

Kids stare the most because they don't know. This little boy asked me, "How did you lose your leg?" I said, "I was sick." He said, "We still love you." That was really cool. Once I was at the mall and had shorts on. This little boy came up to me and put his hand up my shorts leg to see where my leg was. I didn't say anything. I let him do it. Little kids explore, and don't always talk.

If people start talking to me, and then ask me, I tell them. The only people I don't tell are the ones who ask me the wrong way. You aren't supposed to just come out and say, "What happened to your leg?" I don't like people just saying something like that 'cause I don't feel that they asked me the right way. I just walk on and ignore them. You're supposed to say, "If you don't mind me asking, what happened to your leg?" Sometimes people just talk about other things, but you can tell what they are thinking, because they're making a point of not looking down at my missing leg. I'll say something to them about my leg if they don't say something to me first.

Beep, Beep
Mason, 16

I beep whenever I go through a metal detector. The rods in my leg are titanium. They pull me aside and say, "Stand there and don't move." One time we asked the doctor for a note of explanation. He said that it would be so easy for someone to have a fake card that it doesn't mean anything to security people. So they scan me. I don't have to lift up my pant leg. I just tell them that I had surgery in my knee and they scan me and pat me down. When I have shorts on, it's always easier 'cause then they see all the scars.

It's Not the People—It's the Bathrooms
Jonathan, 21

The main problem going out isn't dealing with people—it's the bathrooms. I'll get anxious before we go out, worried that there aren't going to be accessible bathrooms or that people will bump into me accidentally because my wheelchair takes up a lot of space. Sometimes we have to go to several bathrooms before I can find one I can use. Sometimes I can't get into stores because the merchandise racks are so close together. And we can only go to certain movie theaters because I have to lie down in my wheelchair during the movie, and there has to be enough room for that. Sometimes people who aren't handicapped sit in the handicapped places in the movie theaters and don't move. Some of those people make rude comments. It always hurts my feelings.

You just don't know what it's like until you're in that situation. People take a lot for granted. We went to Washington, D.C., to see our senator to talk about my school not being wheelchair accessible, and I had to stay in the van because I couldn't get into the building in my wheelchair. Can you believe that?

Clueless People
Cassidy, 7

People talk about me a lot right in front of me, like I don't exist. I guess they think that because I'm blind, I also can't hear. Or they'll ask me if I know sign language. I'm blind! Worst of all, they'll say mean things about me not having a nose, right in front of me. That makes me feel bad. I'm okay talking about my missing nose, as long as people ask me nicely. I say, "I don't have a nose, but thank you for asking. I was born that way. Everyone has something different about them, mine is just my eyes and my nose."

Nasty People—Shame on You
Kimberlie, 10

When we went to Disney World, we didn't have to stand in lines because we had this special handicap pass to go to the front. This one lady got mad because we got to go to the head of the line. I was riding in a wheelchair because I was really weak. This woman's kids were trampling over everyone to get on this one ride. It was one of the few times that somebody wasn't nice. My mom said nicely to her, "If you don't mind, we'd really like to all stay together please." The woman said something mean to my mom. My mom said to me, "That's not our problem—it's hers."

Some people were really great though. There was a waitress in our favorite restaurant whose granddaughter had leukemia and was going through treatments the same time as me. I wouldn't eat, so she went into the kitchen and whipped up a strawberry-banana smoothie, and I ate the whole thing. There really are some great people out there.

Helping Others Understand

Blayne, 19

Kids especially are so accepting. For the most part I say, "My legs just don't work right. I was born that way." They're like, "Oh, I just wanted to know. That's cool. No big deal."

I'm so okay with my disability that I don't mind questions. But I do get tired of them sometimes. It's one of those things that little kids are just so cute about. They'll say, "Mommy, why does he walk like that?" Mommy's like, "Shut up!" That's what makes me wanna go off. Once I was shopping and I turned around to a lady and said, "Why are you telling him to hush? You're just teaching him not to be curious." The lady was very honest with me and said, "I don't know what to say." I said, "Well, then ask me." We ended up having a long conversation about it. She said to me, "Not all people would be as open and honest as you. Some people would be offended." I said, "Yeah, you're right. I shouldn't have jumped down your throat so fast. I'm sorry. But let me explain." I told her the whole story about me, and then told it in three-year-old terms for her child. He was just curious, not thinking anything was wrong or bad. I've had lots of little kids poke me in the knee to see if I can feel things. It's really neat because I've been able to help kids understand people like me.

I have a little sister who will never again look at a disabled person and have pity. That's because of me. She knows there's nothing to pity. My roommate's son, four years old, doesn't even realize that there's anything different. Just today, he said, "Blayne, chase me!" I said, "I can't." "Why not?" "Remember, I can't run?" "Oh, yeah. I forgot."

Born in a Wheelchair?

Lindsey, 10

I want people to know that I'm more capable of doing things than they think. They think, "Oh, she's in a wheelchair, she can't do this. She can't walk at all." I've had people walk up to me and say, "How'd you break your legs?" They think that, because I'm in a wheelchair, it's just a broken leg. I'm like, "I was born like this." They're like, "You came out of your mommy's tummy in a wheelchair?"

I Know Me

Charon, 18

If somebody said rude things to me, I'd be okay because I already know the person I am. Whatever they say is their opinion. All that matters is how I feel, and how those who love me feel. That's really it. People who don't take the time to know you, but then judge you, aren't worth it. You can't tell rude people how to think. Something bad might happen to them one day, but I wouldn't tell them that. It's not my job to help them.

People Don't Ask Me to Lick Banana Slugs Anymore

Elyse, 13

Before the accident, people used to dare me to do things because I was such a daredevil. Since the accident, they don't do that any more because they think I'm fragile. People used to dare me to do all kinds of things, like lick a banana slug. In Oregon, we have great-big banana slugs in the forests. I discovered that you have to lick the bottom of the banana slug or your tongue will go numb. Actually, I licked the top because the bottom was all dirty, and I wasn't going to lick dirt.

It's funny how people change, but I'm still the same daredevil. The other day, I tasted horse treats. No one dared me to, I just wanted to know what they tasted like. They taste like horse oats, only apple flavor.

Look Out for What Car?

Cassidy, 7

Since I'm blind, someone runs alongside me when I ride my bike so I don't run into things. Or my parents will stand in our driveway and shout directions at me. They'll tell me: slight left or slight right, and turn left or turn right. Then other people will try and help me. They'll say, "Don't hit the car!" "Look out for this . . . look out for that." Saying, "Look out for the car" doesn't help because I don't know where the car is. I'm blind. I have to see the car to be able to look out for it. Some people just don't get it. Telling me to turn left or right, I get that.

Look at Me, Okay?

Blayne, 19

My biggest complaint is that people will look at the person I'm with while talking to me, like they have to make sure that person understands because I can't. I want to grab their face and say, "You're talking to me. Look at me!" Doctors do it a lot. The other day, I was at the Social Security office, and the lady there was actually talking about my case while looking at the woman I had brought with me. My friend stopped the conversation and said, "You should be looking at and speaking to him."

So many people do that to me. It bothers me. My dentist did it to me the other day. I had gone in with my roommate. The dentist asked me if I wanted him to repeat to my roommate what he had done to me. I said, "No, she's just my ride." He did it anyway, while I'm standing right there! He's looking at her the entire time he's talking, telling her details about me. That's always been one of my biggest issues.

Why Wear Shoes if You Can't Walk?

Ryan, 18

A lot of young kids ask why I wear shoes if I'm in a wheelchair and can't walk. I tell them that I still have to protect my feet, even if I don't walk. Sometimes I crawl on the floor to get around. If I didn't have shoes, I would scrape my feet. Even riding in the chair, you could bump or fall. You could break a toe that way. And my feet would get cold.

Everything's Different Now

Abbie, 13

We came out of the restaurant the other night, and there were these junior high girls bebopping around. One of them said, "Look at my arm. I think I have a tumor." You know, just being goofy. We got in the car and my friend said, "Did you hear that girl?" I said, "I heard her." It bothered me. I wanted to say, "I know what a tumor is and you shouldn't joke about it." I see things differently now. I was probably the same way as those girls before I got sick, so I kind of understand. But I relate differently to people now.

I'm Really No Different
Catyche, 20

The first time I went out in public with my wheelchair and oxygen tank, I wasn't worried because I didn't know how it would be. I felt a great sense of freedom. Then I noticed people staring at me. Of course, I hated it. I don't see what's the big deal—it's just a wheelchair. I don't want people to stare or ask questions, or do anything they don't do to other kids. I just wish they would see me as a normal person. People like me are completely normal. We have lives, we have families, and we have hopes and dreams. Don't act as if we're a subspecies that you have to study and ask questions.

Just Freak Them Out!
Blayne, 19

I like having fun with people. It's actually pretty easy if you have any kind of physical issue. My baclofen pump is a fun one—the hockey-puck thing I have under my skin at my waist. It's very apparent that it's there because I'm so thin. I will say, "You want to see something creepy?" Then I'll lift my shirt to show people. They'll be like, "What is that?" A cool thing is that you can actually stick your thumb behind it and you can feel the whole thing. People will be like, "Can I touch it?" I say, "Sure." They'll ask, "Will it hurt?" I'll say, "No, go ahead." They'll slowly try to touch it. Then I'll scream and freak them out.

Look, I'm a Girl
Jessica, 12

People used to think I was a boy because I was bald. So we made a shirt that read: "I Am a Girl" in the front, and on the back "Get Used to It." Before I had the shirt, we were at the store and this old lady was serving samples of pop. She yelled out at my mom, "Is it okay if he can have one?" That made me mad. My mom said, "She may have one." I also have a shirt that says, "I'm Not Having a Bad Hair Day, But a No Hair Day."

Mistaken for Child Abuse
Nadia, 12

One time when I was at the grocery store with my daddy, I was all swollen because of my disease. Someone at the grocery store called the police because they thought he had hit me to make my face swell the way it did. My daddy had to explain to them about my illness.

What's Wrong With You?
Blayne, 19

One of my favorite questions is, "What's wrong with you?" I always say, "Nothing, what's wrong with you?" I love that one. When I was 12 and in a wheelchair at the mall, I went up to a complete stranger and started talking to her about something she was looking at. She turned around and looked at me in the wheelchair and said, "You can talk?" I said, "Lady, I'm very articulate. I just happen to be in a wheelchair." It was one of those "Oh, my God, moments," and I've had a few of them!

I'm Not My Daddy's Son
Amber, 15

I went to the store with one of my friends. A very old couple thought I was a boy. They said, "How are you doing, little boy?" I told them that I was a girl. They were so sorry, they couldn't apologize enough. People who I don't know look at me like "Is that a boy or a girl?" It's because I'm bald from my cancer treatments. Sometimes they'll just stare at me for a long time. I've had people look at me when I go walking into the girl's bathroom and say, "What is that guy doing in this bathroom?" I'll have a skirt on and I know they're thinking, "Why does that guy have a skirt on?" I just look at them and smile. That's all I can do.

Miss Bright Eyes
Aaron, 15

One time after chemo, I lost my eyesight and couldn't see for two weeks. I thought I was going to go blind for good. Then I got my sight back, but my whole eyeball was all red. It was really noticeable. When I went out in public, everyone stared at me. I remember going to a restaurant and sitting by the window. A little girl walked past, stopped, and she was face-to-face with me at the window, just staring at me. Her mom didn't even realize it because she had kept walking. She came back and grabbed her daughter, and then she stared at me. That really made me angry.

People have to understand what it feels like to be stared at all the time. They have to put themselves in that person's shoes and say, "How would I feel if there was something different about me and, everywhere I went, somebody stared at me? Would I like that?"

People Understand Cancer, but Not My Disease
Marian, 16

I don't really like people to know that I have arthritis because most people just don't understand it. A kid with arthritis? They just don't get it. Then after a lot of questions, they still don't understand. Even though cancer is more severe, people understand when you say you have cancer—they know what it is and what you're going through. When you say arthritis, they're like, "Oh, that happens to me. Sometimes my knee hurts." I'm like, "Well, that's not it."

Amusement Parks Are Totally Different When You're Blind
Cassidy, 7

I like to ride the roller coaster. Since I'm blind, it's so much fun for me because I can't see what's coming. Suddenly, you go this way and that way, up and down, and you can't see it coming. Also, you can't see how high you are or how fast you are going. Try it; ride the roller coaster but close your eyes the whole time.

The Questions Not Asked
Ryan, 18

I prefer people to ask questions. Don't point and stare. If you want to know, come up and ask me. I'll tell you. I'm not bitter and I won't bite your head off. A lot of people come up and ask me and my mom, "Why are you in the chair?" Most people assume that it happened recently. They don't see braces or any physical sign to show that I'm disabled, so they think that something just happened to me. You look at someone who shows physical signs of being disabled, and they're like, "Oh, he has a disability, just leave him alone." But with me they are like, "Why are you . . . you know?"

Are You a Robot?
Nadia, 12

This girl at camp saw my dialysis tube that comes out of my body when it fell out of the netting that was holding it under my shirt. My tube is long and hangs down, so I curl it up in the netting around my stomach. The girl was horrified. She screamed, "Are you a robot?" She was about 10. I was so embarrassed that I tried to cover it and explain, but she kept saying that I was a robot. I kept trying to explain, but she wouldn't listen and she didn't believe me. Then she went and told everybody that I was a robot and had a tube in my stomach. I got upset and told one of the adults that I wanted to go home because I felt embarrassed and sad. I cried. They told me to calm down and that I probably wouldn't want to go home 'cause I was gonna have fun that day. I didn't go home. The little girl finally started to listen, and she cried and apologized. I was sad then, but I think it's funny now. Sometimes it's fallen out at school, and I come home laughing about it.

I'm Not Just Being Paranoid
Jonathan, 21

One time we went out for dinner. It was after I couldn't use any of my limbs, and my parents had to feed me. I just knew that these people at the next table were talking about me and laughing. I started crying and couldn't finish my dinner.

We went home and had a family conference. I told my parents, "People were making fun of me and I don't want to go out any more." They said that I couldn't know for sure that the people were talking about me. They might have seen something out the window that was funny to them. They said that people were always going to stare. That's just the way it was. Then they said, "We are a family and we love you very, very much. We are not ashamed of you. We want you to keep going out like you did before. We don't mind feeding you, or doing anything it takes for you because you're our son and we love you." I still didn't want to go out for weeks. Then I realized that just because I couldn't do what they can do, I was still a person. We started going out again. We're all different, that's all.

Don't Need the Pity
Tonya, 20

One time, a little girl was making fun of me 'cause I have to keep my legs crossed under me all the time in my wheelchair. The girl said, "You look kinda crazy sittin' there with your legs all crossed underneath. Why don't you open up your legs?" I said, "Look, go on and leave me alone." That's when my uncle got mad, and he and the girl's mama started yelling at each other.

I don't like going out in public too much 'cause the young 'uns stare at me. They'll ask, "Hey, what's wrong with you?" I say, "Just 'cause I'm in this chair, doesn't mean I'm any different than anybody else. I'm just like you. The only thing is that you walk and I can't." I say it nicely and go on about my business. One girl actually said to me, "I want to be your friend 'cause I feel sorry for you." I told her, "Don't feel sorry for me 'cause I don't want anybody pitying me."

Losing Control
Catyche, 20

I'm not able to wheel myself in my wheelchair because I get tired and out of breath. I usually have someone push. In a wheelchair you really lose control of your life. You're at the mercy of whoever is pushing you, and at the mercy of what the world makes available to you in a wheelchair—because not everything is available to you. A lot of times, you can't get to things or reach things, especially in stores. When we go shopping, it gets frustrating because whoever is pushing stops where they want to stop and not where I tell them to stop. I feel like someone else is controlling my life. If we're shopping for clothes, my mom's really great at pushing me. She'll stop if I want to. But when my sister and my cousin take me, they don't stop when I tell them to, so I can look at a skirt. I'm sure they do it on purpose to aggravate me.

A lot of stores are just hard to get through, especially clothing stores, because the racks are crammed in there right next to each other. If I want to go in the handicapped dressing room, I usually have to wait like a half an hour or so because someone who is *not* handicapped is using it. That really frustrates me. I just don't know why people would use a big stall that's made for wheelchairs.

A lot of times, the handicapped parking places are completely taken up. I didn't realize that there were so many handicapped people until I had to use a wheelchair. Every single spot is always taken up. I think they should have a lot more handicapped places to park. Even the hospital spots are filled up. Before I was in a wheelchair, I'd be like, "Oh, my goodness, look at all these handicapped spaces. Surely they don't need that many." Now that I need them, there really aren't enough of them.

Oh, and this one is my favorite! I went to get a handicapped sign to hang from the rearview mirror. The government building where you get the signs had the handicapped ramp halfway around the building. We had to go around the entire block to get to the ramp!

Wheelchair Denial
Jonathan, 21

I knew about my illness early on. I'd get on the Internet and do research. I'd find out stuff about it, like the various stages of deterioration. We were all in denial. When I got my wheelchair, my dad put it upstairs. I don't blame him; none of us wanted it in the house. Then one day, I fell. I couldn't get around so well. We realized that we couldn't be in denial any more. My dad finally got it down for me. Then I was more mobile. With the wheelchair, we started going to more places where I hadn't been able to walk around before.

Faking It at the Mall
Hope, 12

One day I wanted to go to the mall, but the only way I could go was in a wheelchair. I had never been to the mall in a wheelchair, and I was very embarrassed about it. My friend, Gina, was going to go with me, so we came up with a plan. Since I had an extra leg brace, we decided that Gina would use the extra one and we'd both say we needed wheelchairs. It wasn't as embarrassing for me with Gina in a wheelchair, too. Whenever anyone asked what happened, we would tell them that we got in a really bad jet ski accident. People believed us and started telling us their jet ski accident stories. It was really funny, but I felt kinda guilty for lying.

We did cheers in our wheelchairs because we are both cheerleaders. We'd go into stores and get stuck because a lot of stores aren't wheelchair accessible. Then Gina would forget about having to be in a wheelchair and get out and start walking around like she was fine. I'd be like, "You're supposed to be pretending you're hurt!" She'd start limping again. It was so funny. We followed boys around. We didn't talk to them. They kind of avoided us. They probably thought we were stalking them. The whole experience taught me how to have fun in public with my wheelchair, and not feel so embarrassed about it.

Can't Do Buffets Anymore
Charon, 18

I don't like going to my favorite restaurant anymore because I can't do the buffet with one leg. We went there for my mom's birthday. She had to help me with my tray, and I should have been helping her. I felt bad because I'm sitting with my plate, and she has to get her own food on her birthday.

You Need to Trust Me
Lindsey, 10

I get so frustrated at some amusement parks because they won't let me go on some rides. One time we went on this thing that spins around and around and then it gets higher and higher and then when it gets to the top it just spins. But they wouldn't let me on it because they said I didn't have enough back support because I was in a wheelchair. I was like, "Are you crazy?" I have back support. I'm not the kind of person who sits slumped over all the time. I can sit up straight. It just annoys me when I can't go on a ride 'cause I'm in a wheelchair.

I couldn't go on bumper cars either, because they were afraid that I'd damage my legs. They said that if I got hit my legs would break. I about fainted. I would know if I shouldn't go on a ride. They should trust me.

Produce Aisle Massacre
Elyse, 13

We had a funny experience at this one big grocery store. My mom couldn't push the shopping cart and push me in my wheelchair. We tried different things. I would hold the cart and my mom would push me, kind of like a little choo-choo. But I could only use my one good hand so the cart would be angling. I never got the hang of it. We went to the produce department and we really made a mess there. We bumped into everything. The tomatoes and peaches did not survive. It was the "Produce Aisle Massacre."

It was so bad we switched to the "granny" electric carts. But then I had to go to the bathroom. The electric cart wouldn't fit or turn, and I got stuck in the stall, which was really bad because I was right there but couldn't go to the bathroom. We finally got the cart out after a lot of sheer will and determination, and almost killing my ankle. I don't know how grannies go to the bathroom with those carts.

The Clueless Dentist
Ryan, 18

When you have cerebral palsy, you have certain things that you go through. Some kids have severe overbites or dental problems because of grinding their teeth. Also, a lot of cerebral palsy kids don't have good dental hygiene; they can't brush their teeth because their arms or hands are debilitated.

When I go to the dentist, I always transfer by myself from my wheelchair into the dental chair. Then when I'm all kicked back in the chair, the hygienist moves my wheelchair out of the room because it's a real tight squeeze in there. Then she preps me for the dentist.

One time, the dentist started working on me, and he said, "I'd really like to get some panoramic pictures of your mouth. Come on with me." He took a few steps, and I'm just lying there. It was just me and the dentist. The dentist said, "We need to go down this way to take the pictures." He took a few more steps, turned again, and said firmly, "You have to get up and come with me."

I never said a word. I was as red as can be. I was only eight, and I thought, "You're the dentist. You should know all about me and my history, so you should know that I'm in a wheelchair." Finally, the nurse came around the corner, and brought my wheelchair. The dentist was mortified; he apologized up one side and down the other.

A Blowout at the Baptism
Jonathan, 21

The Sunday I got baptized, I had a blowout from the tire of my wheelchair in the middle of church. It was really loud and sounded like a gunshot. Everyone actually ducked. It was so embarrassing. I got really upset because I really wanted to get baptized. We didn't see how that was going to happen since my wheelchair couldn't move.

My dad told the pastor that there was no way we could baptize me today because of the flat tire on my chair. The pastor told us that he wouldn't let us down. He said that we have strong men in this church. They lifted me up, wheelchair and all, and carried me to the pool. I got baptized that day!

Blowout at the Holocaust Museum

Lindsey, 10

The last time we went to Washington, D.C., for the anti-bullying convention, we went to see the Holocaust Museum. I had read novels about kids who survived the Holocaust. We had just gone through a railcar example in the museum. It was dark and sobering and real still and quiet. The next thing we knew, the inner tube in my wheel burst. It sounded like a gunshot and everybody started to panic. Of all places, the Holocaust Museum! Your emotions are on edge anyway. My mom just quickly shouted out, "It's only a wheelchair tire!"

Fun with My Talking Computer

Alan, 20

Because I can't totally speak, I use a portable computer to communicate. I type what I want to say, and I can show the words on-screen or play it in a voice I choose. I don't like it when people try to finish my sentence as I'm typing, so I make up a different ending to the sentence to fake them out.

I also have a bunch of different sounds on the computer, like a buzzer, a doorbell, and a siren. I'll play the doorbell at home and someone will go to the door and look. I have a child's voice that goes "Uh oh." It's really annoying. When I play it, people look around for a child.

I love to play jokes on people and pull pranks with all the creepy voices. I mess with the teacher in my weight-lifting class. One day we were checking body fat using a caliper that pinches your skin. I programmed my computer to say, "Ouch, that hurts!" When the teacher pinched me with the caliper, I hit the voice button on the computer, and she jumped and reacted like she hurt me.

I Need to Wear a Helmet

Elyse, 13

I have been pushed by people who do not have a wheelchair driving license. They always run into things, like walls and corners, or they take corners too fast or too sharp, or they stop too quickly. I can get smashed around pretty good in the wheel-chair. I've had bruises galore, twisted and sprained my ankle, and been dumped out on the sidewalk because of a crack in the sidewalk. I need a helmet in my wheelchair. I want to learn how to ride a dirt bike. It's gotta be safer than being in a wheelchair!

Once Around the Block
Jonathan, 21

One day I told my dad, "I want to go around the block." He asked me if I meant to go around the paths in back of the house. They had made these winding paths level through the pine trees so I could wheel myself through the trees. I told him, "No, I mean around the real block. Down the road, by myself." I rarely did that. I knew my parents were concerned. I wanted to do something on my own—just for myself.

I knew things were happening inside me, and I didn't know how much time I had to live. I had to go around the block one last time, by myself. My dad knew how important it was for me and said, "Okay, if you're not back soon. I'll check on you." I was fine. I did it a few more times, just to know for sure that I could do it. I felt an overwhelming feeling of accomplishment. People in wheelchairs know what I mean about this.

I Heard That
Blayne, 19

People think that you're deaf when you're handicapped. They'll talk about you when they're standing right behind you. They'll say, "Oh, that kid's slow. What's wrong with him?" I'll say, "I can hear you. I heard that." For me, it's more than just ignorance, it's rude! They don't have an understanding for people like me. I'm just going about my life, just like they are.

Chapter 8
Special Memories and Special Friends

"Friends for 20 minutes, brothers for life."
—Charon

"My wheelchair is practically legs." —Lindsey

"Cancer makes me appreciative of what I have and what I don't have." —Miriam

---

There are some benefits to being us—meeting celebrities, free trips, kittens and puppies, and eating whatever we want because, hey, at least we're eating. We have some great memories that we get to share with those we love. Also, when you spend a lot of time in the hospital, you make friends with other kids who are dealing with a lot of the same things. These memories and friendships are precious, and often very different from what other kids experience.

Make-A-Wish Is the Best
Kimberlie, 10

The Make-A-Wish Foundation does a terrific job of helping you escape for your wish. For my wish, we went to Disney World. They really took good care of us. The Magic Kingdom was a little overwhelming because there is so much to see. But we saw everything we could. I loved buying and trading Disney pins with all the Disney employees. A lot of people just gave me pins because they knew I was on my Make-A-Wish trip. We also saw Sea World and Discovery Coast where I swam with the dolphins.

There was just so much to visit and see. It was the best vacation ever. This trip was very important to us as a family because we got to be together and not think about my illness.

Rascal Flats and Other Celebrities
Autumn, 11

Because of my cancer, I get special things that are really cool. I got to meet Rascal Flats, my favorite country music band. I got to go onstage and introduce them twice at their concerts, and I got their autographs. After I introduced them, they called me back onstage and sang the first song to me. It was so cool. They even called me when I was in the hospital.

All Those Cards Are Great
Hope, 12

I have so many stuffed animals and so many gifts. I have every Hallmark card ever made, like around five copies of each. I have a box full of cards and each one of them means the world to me.

Groovin' with the Panthers
Charon, 18

I love football, and the Carolina Panthers are my favorite team. Steve Smith is my favorite player. I met him after Amy, the Child Life specialist at the hospital, got game tickets for me and two friends, which included passes to go on the field. Steve Smith came over and started talking to me. I have pictures of him and me. I met a lot more players and also the cheerleaders.

The Newspaper Article
Marian, 16

Most people don't know that I have arthritis. My doctor wanted me to be interviewed in our local paper because, even with arthritis, I'm still pretty good at high jumping. People don't understand how I can have arthritis and be on the track team. My doctor wanted me to do the article to show people what we can really do, and to inspire others.

The article talked about what I've gone through with my arthritis and the medications I'm on. It also talked about me going to the state finals for high jumping. They interviewed my track coach, who talked about how well I was doing. My close friends were like, "I'm so proud of you!" It made me feel good.

Ah, the Service
Hope, 12

When I was really sick at home, I had 24-hour service from my mother. She would sleep on the couch upstairs to be close by. My mom waited on me hand-and-foot. I could have anything I wanted for dinner. Also, I got a second kitten because of my cancer. I'm still playing the illness to get a Chinese crested dog or a lab puppy. As soon as we hear the "R word" (remission), I'll get the dog. When my mom and I get in a fight and she says, "I'm not going to wait on you!" I'll say, "I've got a million moms I could call." They all cook me food (although it's not always food I recognize).

Jeter and Goofy
Miriam, 19

I met the Yankees this past summer. Cherish Creations gave me that. I met Derek Jeter. When he came up to me, I was like, "Hi, Mr. Jeter, could you sign my jersey?" He did. I told him, "I'm legal. I know how to cook and I know how to clean. Do you want to get married?" He said, "You're cute." He gave me a kiss on my cheek. His sister also had Hodgkin's like me.

Make-A-Wish gave me a trip to Florida. We went to Disney World and I met Goofy. That was my moment. I got his autograph. I checked off my two top "to do" things—Goofy and Jeter. My next "to do" is to get a college degree.

Autumn's Song and Autumn's Day
Autumn, 11

I wished for a trip to Nashville to meet Tim McGraw and Faith Hill. My mom wrote a song called, "On My Knees," which was my favorite song before I got diagnosed. Every time we get in the car I have my mom play it. I knew it word for word. I wanted to have Tim McGraw and Faith Hill record it just for me. After I was diagnosed, my mom rewrote it. She only had to change a few words and it became, "Autumn's Song." But Tim and Faith couldn't sing it for me. Their management company said that, because of some legality, they could only record songs that were their own songs. But Tim McGraw's drummer, Dave Dunkley, sang it. We've got it on a CD—a song that my mom wrote for me and that a famous person sang.

I've had a lot of blessings. The town of Kings Mountain had "Autumn's Day." They took me on a hot air balloon ride, took me around on a fire truck, and had me up at the city hall. The mayor took us all out to eat with the chief of police and the fire chief.

I'm a Movie Star
Lindsey, 10

I was in a movie called *The Angel Doll*. It was about a girl with polio, so they needed a little girl who was experienced with crutches and a wheelchair. I was the co-star and I had to memorize lines. I was six, and I played a four-year-old who was dying. The story was based on Jerry Bledsoe's childhood friendship with a boy whose little sister had polio. The brother searched for an angel doll to give to his dying sister at Christmas. I thought, "This is so cool. I'll actually see myself on TV." It's on video now. It won awards, and is usually on television around Christmas time.

I Would Rather Be Normal
Catyche, 20

There are advantages to being sick, but they don't make up for being sick. If you're fighting with your siblings, you can win no matter what the argument because you have the ultimate trump card. Being sick, I get unexpected gifts, like two free computers, extensions on homework assignments, free sketchbooks and other books, candy, and special opportunities, like being part of this book.

In the fifth grade I was looking forward to a class trip to see *Phantom of the Opera* on Broadway. I was so excited to go, and then I got pneumonia. It was one of the bad ones, too, and they wouldn't let me go. But they called Make-A-Wish, who gave me a computer and tickets to see *Beauty and The Beast* on Broadway. It was so amazing. I'm so grateful.

The gifts and all don't outweigh the problems that I have with sickle cell. There's no way to even come close. I would go without all those gifts if I could just be normal.

Chemo Pup
Kimberlie, 10

On the last day of school last year, I went to my friend's pool party. I held and petted her new puppy the whole time I was there. My friend's dad told us that there were other puppies that we should check out at the pet shop. We went to the pet store. When we walked in, a worker asked if I was Kimberlie. I said, "Yes," and she told me that someone had purchased a puppy for me and that I could pick out any puppy I wanted. The employee said that the person wanted to remain anonymous.

I was so happy. I can't even start to explain the feelings. My mom, sister, and I all started to cry because it was such a kind thing to do. I held all the puppies and chose a tan and white Boston terrier/Chihuahua mix that I named Buttercup the Chemo Pup. He makes me laugh because he goes psycho—running around the house really fast and running into things—just being crazy. Crazy is good!

Camp in Aspen
Sarah, 11

I did a once-in-a-lifetime trip to Aspen, Colorado. It was through the Silver Lining Foundation that was started by ex-pro tennis player Andrea Yeager. She had always loved visiting kids in the hospital, and had a special place in her heart for cancer kids. She, along with other celebrities, started a ranch. All summer they invite people from hospitals to camp. I was at the big, beautiful ranch for a week for swimming, riding horses, playing games, and having fun. You can only go once, but you can come back as a counselor when you're older. I want to do that.

Something to Remember Forever
Amber, 15

Make-A-Wish gave us a cruise to the Bahamas. A limousine picked us up and took us to the airport. I had never been in a limousine, or on a plane, or on a cruise. It was a five-day cruise, and I didn't get seasick. I went jet skiing with Daddy. I got to raise the Make-A-Wish flag that read, "Wishes at Sea." We got to eat with the captain one night, and we met a lot of nice people. This man who never knew us walked up to Mama and said, "You are an inspiration. I've watched you and your husband with your children, and ya'll are just pure inspiration. You've touched my heart. You just don't know." I know that on that cruise, we touched a lot of people's hearts.

I want to help people, too. I hope that somehow we'll be able to help other families. We want them to have what we had. We were so stressed out when we went on this trip. When we came back, I just felt like so much had been relieved. For those few days away from everything, we had all forgotten my cancer. I even forgot what was wrong with me.

European Vacation
Mason, 16

I got a trip to Europe from the Children's Wish Foundation. My mom is from Germany and all of her family is over there. What's interesting is that our family in Germany asked a lot of questions about my cancer and how things are done in America, which was cool with me. We have family and friends all over Germany, and one of Dad's best friends has a farm in Switzerland where we stayed for a time. We went to Germany, Switzerland, and Italy. It was amazing. It was such a great trip.

Kidney Camp
Nadia, 12

I went to Kidney Camp. The kids were all different ages, but we all had something going on with our kidneys. They had dialysis machines there for all of us. They had a beach and a water park with waterslides. We swam, did arts and crafts, and rode horses. The best part of all is that they gave us food that we shouldn't eat, like pizza and hot dogs, because of our kidney problems. I felt more comfortable at camp than around school with regular friends because everyone at camp knew what you're going through.

Hospital Friends
Autumn, 11

The nurses called me "The Ambassador," because I would always make friends with the other kids in the hospital, and get them out of their rooms. If there was a kid who was sad and wouldn't do activities, they'd call me in.

Making friends with kids in the hospital is so different from your other friends. A friend who has cancer knows exactly how you feel. Meeting my best friend, Sarah, in the hospital was great. One day in the playroom, we started talking. We played together and were in each other's rooms all the time. We became instant friends and have been buddies ever since.

I had another friend, Emily, who had AML, the worst of all leukemias. Emily didn't make it. She was a year older than me, and I loved her. I looked up to her. Emily was a permanent fixture at the hospital. Every time I went in, I made sure to visit Emily. When Emily died, it was sad because I knew her for a very, very long time. I still miss her very much and it makes me sad. Emily was the first friend I lost. She was like my big sister.

Comparing Treatments
Jessica, 12

Having friends who are sick like you is nice because you can talk to them and compare experiences. You can't do that with your other friends; except tell them what you go through and hope they understand. If I try to explain things to my regular friends, like blood counts, they just go, "Huh?" My friends who have cancer understand about counts and treatment. We can easily talk about what we go through. We even compare what it's like at different hospitals.

An ESPN Story on Me (Okay, I Wasn't the Whole Story)
Mason, 16

After my dad tried to contact Lance Armstrong to tell him how he had inspired me, a writer at the Lance Armstrong Foundation said *ESPN The Magazine* was writing an article on Lance. They wanted to know if it was okay to talk with me. This was about the time of my sixth treatment. The writer wanted to know how Lance had inspired me.

Lance, for me, is about knowledge, information, research, and strength. He's more than an artifact or idol to me. I admire his strength and what he's overcome. They used my story and picture in the article. They gave my link to my Caring Bridge Web site, which is a great organization. Through the ESPN article link, people were able to contact us, encourage me, and tell me how I inspired them.

Then the best of all things happened. This past October, I was the only kid in the country who was selected to ride with Lance in his annual "Ride for the Roses" in Austin, Texas. I actually rode alongside Lance! It was the most incredible experience.

My Friend, Terri
Catyche, 20

My friend Terri is a little older than me and has sickle cell. I met her in the hospital when I was in the ICU after waking up from a seizure. I was in so much pain and felt so hopeless. The doctors couldn't do anything to control the pain. They were afraid that I'd seizure again if they gave me more drugs.

So my doctor got Terri to speak to me. She talked to me the whole day. She was amazing. She ordered food and we ate together. I kept drifting in and out of consciousness. When I was awake, I would talk to her. I felt like there was one other person who had the same problems as me. Her sickle cell was as bad as mine. She gets really sick, too. She's had some three-month hospitalizations, which is worse than me. I felt so bad for her because she didn't have her family with her and had to spend every night alone. Her father is in Jamaica, and her mother remarried and just doesn't seem to care. I am fortunate that I never have to spend the night by myself at the hospital.

Hey, They're Just Like Me
Aaron, 15

When you have friends who have cancer, you never have to repeat yourself, and you don't have to describe anything to them. You say, "My stomach hurts because I just had chemo," and they know what kind of pain you have. If you say, "I'm sick of being in the hospital all the time," you don't have to explain yourself. They know exactly what's going on. You can't understand it until you have been through it. Once you've been through it, you understand without even talking about it.

You relate to different people in different ways—but never in just one way. Like Joyce and me, we both relate to our cancer. But we don't just sit around talking about cancer. Sometimes Joyce gets really sad. I tell her how special she is, how strong she is, how brave she is, how much I love her, and that everything is going to be okay. We'll both get emotional and then she hugs me and says she loves me.

Two Kinds of Friends
Kimberlie, 10

It feels good to know other kids who really understand all that you are going through. It's not that your other friends are not kind or don't try to understand, it's just that they can't really understand it unless they have been through it. It feels good to have both kinds of friends because it's nice to be able to talk about hospital stuff, but it is also nice to *not* talk about hospital stuff!

They Already Knew
Marian, 16

What helped the most, I think, is an event we went to several years ago in Seattle. I was in sixth grade, and the event lasted three days. When everyone in the group first met, we didn't really talk about having arthritis. But then, we started talking about it a lot more once we got to know each other. I was with all these other girls who had the same symptoms as me. I remember how nice it felt to relate to them more than to others. I remember it was really fun for me just to be with those people because they immediately understood, and I didn't have to explain anything. They already knew how it was.

A Shea Christmas
Charon, 18

Last Christmas, the Shea brothers of Shea Homes came to my hospital room with gifts. They wanted to do an entire Christmas for us, complete with presents for everyone in my family and a great meal. So they came to our house with a lot of their employees, and they brought all this great food and all these presents. They gave us one of the most memorable Christmases we've ever had. It was so unbelievable. They were just all so nice and friendly to us. We really loved that they did this for a family they had just met.

My Little Yellow Surprise
Amber, 15

One day Mama said, "We need to go out to eat because I just don't feel like cooking." So we went to our local burger joint. I was gonna sit with one of my best friends who was there, but Daddy said, "No, I want you sitting over here with me." We were just sitting there talking and drinking our tea when I heard a horn blowing. I looked out the window and this car was coming at us really fast. I didn't think it was going to stop. It was a yellow Volkswagen that finally came to a stop. When I looked in the passenger window there was a sign that read "Looking for Amber." I started crying. My mouth dropped and my head dropped, and Daddy thought I had passed out. I had been talking about wanting a yellow Volkswagen. It had a red bow on it and a frog tied from the rearview mirror. I love stuffed frogs.

Mason Is Like a Brother
Charon, 18

When I first went in the hospital, the nurses always talked about Mason. They said, "We have a 15-year-old who has osteosarcoma. He's a baseball player." I didn't get to meet him for two months because both of us were always so sick, or we weren't in the hospital at the same time. Finally, I got to meet him. He's like my brother now. We are real, real close, and for more reasons than us both having cancer. It was that at first, but now it's because of so many other things. It's a guy thing. We have a lot of things in common, like baseball. We like doing some of the same stuff. We'd be best friends with or without the cancer.

My Pal, Charon
Mason, 16

One of my best friends I met in the hospital, Charon, is a year older than me. He had osteosarcoma in his femur, right above his left knee. He had the same doctors and was going through the exact same thing I was, but was one month behind me in treatments. He has seven brothers and sisters, and I have one brother. I'm white and live in the city, and he's black and lives in the country.

I met Charon because my dad talked to him. My dad had been asking the nurses if there were any kids my age who were in the hospital for whatever reason. Charon was 17 and we both like the Yankees. Last year, when the Yankees were playing the Red Sox, we watched all the games together in the hospital.

I knew Charon was going up for surgery to remove his leg, and I knew he was nervous and scared. I wrote him a letter saying things like, "Be strong and everything's gonna be okay. You'll be fine. I know you'll be fine." I felt bad for him and tried to be as supportive as I could. He was worried about losing his leg, but I think he was more worried about the cancer. I told him that after my surgery I felt a great relief in knowing that the cancer was gone and out of my body. I told him, at least then you will be relieved and done with it. The cancer will be gone, but losing a leg is a tough thing.

After the surgery, he seemed okay with it. He was surprisingly upbeat. He was out of bed on crutches after two days. I felt bad for him 'cause he was alone for the most part. It was just his mom visiting when she could, but she had to work all the time; and they lived an hour away from the hospital. His brothers would seldom visit him. Dad would always drop in on him and find out what he and his family needed. Mom (and some of her friends) arranged for a great Christmas for him and his family.

When Charon and I hung out, we just talked about stuff that interested us. We talked a little about our illnesses, but mostly other things. The friendship really developed the summer we went to the Silver Lining Camp in Aspen. We really bonded. The fact that we both had cancer is not really why we are friends. I guess that's kind of a factor, but it's not a big one. At first, it was our reason for talking. It's sort of an undercurrent when you're in the hospital. Now, cancer doesn't come up in the conversation.

Like a War Zone
Justin, 12

I made friends in the hospital. About half of the children on the bone marrow unit died, and that was really hard. When you are in the hospital so long, they become like your family. It was weird because some kids would be doing fine, and you'd think for sure that they would be the survivors. Then one week later you find out they had passed away. Other kids were so sick and fragile, you'd think there was no way they could live, but they do. You just couldn't predict. It was like a war zone.

Pray with Hope

Hope, 12

I have these stickers that were made for me to put on cars. They say "Pray with Hope" with a heart around "Hope." When we go driving around the city, I see all these stickers on cars and I think, "Oh, my God, all these people care enough to put my stickers on their cars." It really makes me feel good.

Chapter 9

I Can Do Anything You Can Do

"I can do pretty much what I want to do. I can't think of anything that I can't do." —Meredith

"Even when I'm sick, I feel like I can do anything anyone else could do, only better." —Sarah

"You are only bound by what you think you can't do." —Blayne

Although our bodies give us problems and we have our share of ups and downs, we can do anything you can do. Here are things that we have accomplished, like making a difference in the world because we're on committees and hold offices. We are athletic, artistic, and inventive. We are determined to leave our mark on the world. We do lots of things that would amaze you.

The Only Limits Are in Your Head

Blayne, 19

I always hated having to sit on the sidelines while my classmates played kickball in the summer. I'd put on a smiley face and pretend I was having fun. But I wasn't—it sucked! It wasn't until I realized, "Hey, I don't care if I get my pants dirty, I'm getting out there, too." And I did! I played kickball and had fun, too! You gotta go for it and take chances!

That was when I said, "I'd love to go bowling." It's turned out to be one of my favorite things to do. I suck at it because I have to get on my knees and push the ball, but I have a blast. I don't care if I hit a single pin.

I've been down to the Eight Caves. They're underground caves that are full of boulders, and people who are able-bodied have trouble getting down there. What I had to do (thank goodness for the Americans with Disabilities Act), was tell them that they needed to send a park ranger down with me. My canes were useless. The park ranger held me by the waist every step I took. I'd take a step and he made sure I was okay, then I took another step and then another. It took us four and a half hours to get all the way to the back.

Do you know how many people with cerebral palsy have been down to Eight Caves? Just me! The only limits you have are those in your head.

> "The world will tell you who you are, until *you* tell the world who you are."
> —*Blayne*

My Goal Is to Save Horses

Lindsey, 10

I'd like to be a large animal vet. I want to help horses. A lot of people put horses to sleep because they think that when they have a broken leg they're not going to make it. You can't exactly put a cast on a horse. I want to find a cure for that to save horses from being slaughtered. When race horses get lame, they are sent to a slaughtering place, and then they turn their hooves into glue.

Rock Climbing

Cassidy, 7

"I'm not afraid of anything; okay, except thunder-storms." —*Cassidy*

I'm not afraid of anything. I went rock climbing, and the best thing I did was fall. I love to fall wearing the harness. I knew I must have been really high up. I twirled while I was falling. When you're blind and you rock climb, you can't really see how high you are.

Inventions and Patents

Scotty, 11

Me and my friend Jeremy are working on something that we want to patent. It is a soccer ball thing that measures how hard you kick the ball. We're still working on it. I also want to invent a needle that gives shots automatically and doesn't hurt. That's why I need to go through college. I'm always thinking of things to invent.

A Singing Doctor

Autumn, 11

When I grow up, I want to be an orthodontist, because they make a whole bunch of money. I'm going to have to wear braces soon. I also want to be a country singer and a pediatric oncologist. My parents laughed and told me, "Well, you could be a singing doctor." My parents bought me karaoke and a microphone. I use it a lot, and I put on shows in the hospital. I even wrote up posters saying "Now Appearing . . . " When I'm in my hospital room singing and dancing, all the nurses, patients, and parents stand in the hall listening.

A Different Path Can Be Rewarding

Catyche, 20

I always thought I wanted to work in science, most likely medicine. But after I spent so much time in the hospital, I didn't think I could work in a hospital. So I decided to be a veterinarian. I love animals. I would love to work with lions, or whales and dolphins. But I don't think I'll be able to do it because to be a vet you have to be a doctor. You have to be on call, and you have to spend a certain amount of time in the hospital standing up. I also thought about being a wildlife biologist, but you have to be very athletic, like walk mountainsides to collect data. I can't do that, at least for now.

That was really hard for me—giving up my dreams. I was angry and frustrated. One of the most important things that helped turn my mindset around was when my aunt said, "It's not only you. A lot of people, when they start out in life, have this idea of what they're going to be and what they're going to do. But life just takes its toll, and they follow a different path. There is nothing good or bad about that. Just because you choose something else doesn't mean it's going to be less fulfilling or rewarding."

I Had to Change My Plans
Alan, 20

Before my coma, I was planning on becoming a doctor. I was planning on going to Creighton for pre-med and then to Johns Hopkins University. But that changed. John, my caregiver, always thought I would be better off going to Stanford University and becoming a writer. He thought I would be a better writer than a doctor. I plan to get my degree in English. I would like to be a professional writer. I've always written short stories. My favorite writer is Charles Bukowski. I want to write poetry. I wrote a version of a Bukowski poem as it relates to my life. These are my accomplishments so far: I had a newspaper column in the high school paper my senior year. I had two poems published in the high school poetry book. I am featured on a Web site showing how I use my Mercury augmentative computer. I received a scholarship for college tuition.

Running with Horses
Blayne, 19

I have been riding horses for therapy for about five years. It's so cool that I can't even describe it. When I was 16, I remember looking down at my shadow as I was riding and saying to my mom, "I look normal. I look just like anybody else who's sitting on a horse." Then the first time I rode a horse on the beach it was so liberating. I remember saying, "I'm running!"

When I walk, I feel like I walk just like everyone else. It doesn't feel like I walk any differently until I walk past a mirror. Then I automatically straighten up because I think, "Does it really look like that!" Not that I'm ashamed of it, but it just doesn't feel like I walk like that.

So being able to look at the shadow with me sitting on the horse looking "normal" was just amazing. My mother was behind me crying. I had no idea until a year later that it touched her as much as it did.

I've done everything that doctors told me I'd never be able to do. First it was, "You'll never walk." Then it was, "You'll never run." Well, I didn't run on my own two feet, but I found a way to do it on a horse!

I told my doctor last year, "I want to go bungee jumping." He said, "Okay." I said, "Will I hurt anything?" He said, "Go for it!" So I went bungee jumping for graduation. I loved it!

I Like Me
Lindsey, 10

> "You have to be happy with yourself, because you can't change it." —*Lindsey*

I'm happy with the way I am, and a lot of people notice me because of the wheelchair. I guess they think I need help. They don't realize I'm more independent than most kids in a wheelchair, but I still like people to try and help me. I don't think there's anything different about me except for the fact that I use a wheelchair. I do almost everything that everybody else does.

Sports and Being Blind
Cassidy, 7

I play golf, even though I'm blind. Someone points me in the direction, tells me how far the hole is, and how hard to hit. Last time I played, I won some holes, and I was playing against kids who could see! I also play basketball. I feel the ball going in the hoop. Someone lifts me on his shoulders, or we play with the little kids hoop. I also dribble the ball. I want to play soccer, but my mom thinks it's too rough. I've been begging to play soccer. I have this soccer ball that beeps after you kick it so I can find it.

A Dare Devil and a Good Speller
Elyse, 13

I like to play Scrabble because I can spell really good (not to brag or anything). I can usually beat the other player. I know how to spell "antidisestablishmentarianism," which means being against the separation between the church and state. I also won my class spelling bee. I qualified to go to the state championship, but I was actually in a coma when the championship took place. It would have been hard for me to spell in a coma.

Even after what I've been through, I still try to have everything the same and try to do the same things as before the accident. My parents let me do things, like other kids, even though I might get hurt. I've been on this big swing where they harness you in and you go flying around. I've always loved this kind of stuff. It's like bungee jumping. My mom says I have this daredevil personality. I did all this before my accident; and I still do it. Nothing is going to slow me down.

Get Out of My Way
Lindsey, 10

I play wheelchair basketball. We use a wheelchair called a "sports chair." It's basically a lightweight chair and the wheels are tilted instead of being straight. It helps you turn sharper. It doesn't have brakes. But it has a ton of seatbelts so you don't fall out, and a bumper to protect you if you ram people on defense. My team is called the Buzzer Beaters. We don't have a regular season because there aren't enough wheelchair basketball teams in the United States, so we have three or four tournaments a year. The teams are coed, and there are some pretty aggressive boys.

In the first tournament, I thought I smelled smoke, and I was in a panic. It was from the wheelchairs ramming. You could actually see the sparks, that's how hard they hit. The first time I got hit, I was shocked. The first year everybody was always saying, "Sorry" if they hit you, but now we scream, "Get out of my way!"

Having One Leg Isn't That Different
Charon, 18

People are weird. They don't think I can do anything since I got my leg amputated. I went back to school as soon as possible after my operation. My friends were like, "Why do you wanna get back to school so quick?" I said, "Trust me, you'd be the same way if you were sitting alone in the hospital." They ask me how I deal with having one leg. I just deal with it. But some people don't know how it is. They're like, "How do you take a shower?" I say, "How do you take a shower? I take it the same way you do." They think, because I have one leg, I can't do the normal stuff. I can't run like them, but I can fly on my crutches.

A Pediatrician
Mason, 16

Even before I got ill, I wanted to be a pediatrician. Since I got sick, I've definitely thought about being a pediatric oncologist. I think it would be great working with kids. It would be tough, but it definitely would be rewarding telling a kid that they did not have to come back to the hospital. Also, with teenagers, since I went through the same thing, I could communicate with them and make them feel comfortable.

I'm Like a T-Rex
Justin, 12

When I grow up, I definitely do not want to be a doctor. I have a lot of experience with medicine, and I want to avoid it. I know way too much about cancer. I've wanted to be an animal trainer, and in the FBI. In our home gym, I'm working on being more muscular. I don't have that much endurance, but I'm working on it. I'm like a T-rex—I can run fast for short distances. I'd be terrible at track, unless it's sprints. Other than that, I think I can do anything anyone else can do.

We All Scream for Ice Cream and Fame
Sarah, 11

When I was younger, I wanted to be famous, like an actor, singer, dancer, or whatever. I've acted some. I took dancing. I don't mind being in front of people.

As my first job, I'd like to be someone who dishes out ice cream and makes other people happy. Then I'll go from there. I still want to be famous. But selling ice cream as my first job would be perfect. I could save money so I could buy a car. I'd go buy a car and drive to Hollywood and be famous.

Horseplay
Meredith, 10

I've been riding horses since I was two. It's great therapy. When I first started riding, I was very stiff. But now when I get off the horse, I am much more limber. That really helps because I can then do my stretches at home better. I ride Western style, and I have my own horse named Levi. I got him for my birthday a few months ago. After I get off now, it's hard to walk because I have "horse legs." It's when your legs are wobbly. If you haven't ridden in a while, and then you ride for an hour or so, your legs are wobbly. You're using leg muscles to guide the horse. I've fallen off my horse, but I get right back on.

I Play My Own Music
Cassidy, 7

I've been playing the piano since I was three. I started taking lessons when I was four because we couldn't find an instructor who would take me at three. I play by ear because I'm blind and can't read music. I have a guitar, too, but it only has one string. I've been begging to play the guitar and the harp. Once, this guy was playing a harp in the park, and he let me play. After 10 minutes of touching the strings, I played "Amazing Grace." I pick a song and then I sing it. I figure out how to play the song on the piano just by listening. I try the piano keys until I find the right one that makes the right noise. I can hear a song and then play it, and I can break a song apart and listen to just the melody or the harmony.

Chapter 10

Back at You

"Attitude is a huge part of life, and going with the flow." —Luke

"Some people take life for granted. I don't." —Amber

"It's not a given that you go through an experience and learn from it. You have to reflect on that experience and say, 'What can I learn from it?" —Blayne

---

So many people have been there for us that we really appreciate the people in our lives. We've been helped by family, friends, doctors, nurses, charitable groups, and sometimes even complete strangers. So we know it's important to give back. We help other kids in the hospital, go on speaking tours at schools, do fund-raising through car washes, bake sales, ballroom galas, and barbecues—whatever it takes—even putting our thoughts and advice in this book to help others get through what we've gone through. Maybe you'll get some ideas here and experience that cool feeling of giving back.

Pretty People CAN Have Cancer
Miriam, 19

I was in the hospital watching television and thinking about the television actors. They are the beautiful people, and you hardly ever see any of their characters sick or in a wheelchair. Then I saw this one show where one character had cancer. That was so amazing. It really got me. That's when I decided what I wanted to do.

I've never worked my cancer to get things, but I think I'll work it when it's time for me to get a job on television. I'm a bit of a drama queen—I realized that at a very early age. I need to use that to help others. As soon as I get healthy and get out of here, I want to work on television and help kids with cancer by educating the world about how we are just regular people. Also, I'm gonna go to schools and talk about treating people with the same respect I was shown in school. My class saw me go through my transformation. I wasn't a "freak" to them. It was normal—they got a cold or broken arm, I happened to get cancer—we survived high school together.

I want to go out and educate people of all ages. That's my focus in life.

I Have Impact
Blayne, 19

I've always had the ability to have a positive impact on other people because I've been through so much. Sure I went through, "Oh, my God, my life is changing. I don't know what I'm gonna do." But after a while, you kinda internalize it and say, "Okay, how can I make this work? How can I change this? What can I learn from this?" It wasn't until I was 15 that I started to not hate God so much for this whole thing, and I said, "You know, this can be the biggest learning tool I have ever seen." I really did turn it around.

I have been a camp counselor for a disabled youth camp every summer. It's called Sunshine for the Physically Challenged Foundation. It is a completely wheelchair-accessible camp in Washington. They match up kids with varying disabilities, from ages 5 to 18, with teen counselors. I had planned on going to the camp as a camper. They told me, "You know, Blayne, you don't really qualify. Each kid has his own counselor, but you don't really need that type of help. But we could sure use your skills as a counselor! We have a young, deaf man who's also in a wheelchair, and we'd love for you to be his counselor."

The young man turned out to be eight years old—and he is my inspiration in every sense of the word. Although it was like the blind leading the blind, it was one of the most amazing experiences that I ever had. He was the happiest young man that I ever met in my life. As much as I thought I knew, I just learned so much from him. He was so insightful!

Giving Away My Wish
Hope, 12

I did an unselfish thing that made me famous, which is way cool. When the Make-A-Wish Foundation asked me what my wish was, I felt that I'd already been very blessed with my life. Plus, I found out that there were 155 kids in my area on the waiting list because there wasn't enough money to grant their wishes. So, my wish was to grant the wishes of the 155 kids on the Make-A-Wish waiting list. I always wanted to be famous, like a model, actress, or even the first female United States president. Also, I want to have my own television show called "Hoprah." But I got really famous by being unselfish! I was the first kid in Make-A-Wish history who ever gave away her wish to other kids.

The wish granters were speechless! They had never heard such a wish. It meant raising a million dollars. I said, "What, is that hard?" We decided that one of the ways to raise the money would be to have a huge party. We threw a big formal gala called "The Celebration of Hope." I got to plan everything and made it a "Rat Pack" theme like from the 1940s. Kevin Donnalley, a Carolina Panthers player who played in Super Bowl XXXVIII, agreed to be my date for the party. We raised the money in five weeks, which meant that all the kids who had been waiting for wishes finally got their wishes! It was the most money ever raised for Make-A-Wish by one person. I was on TV and the radio, and the newspaper wrote about it! It was so cool.

I Want to Be Like Hope
Amber, 15

I got my wish from Make-A-Wish because of Hope. We were talking to Amy of Make-A-Wish, and I was telling her something that touched her heart and she said, "Let me make you cry." She told us about Hope. I just hate that we didn't get to meet Hope before she died. She had osteosarcoma, just like me. I wanted so badly to meet another teenager who had osteosarcoma.

I know Hope got my wish granted. I want to finish helping get her wish granted, which is to grant the wishes of other kids. It would make me feel good 'cause Hope worked so hard to grant the wishes of the other kids. I'm organizing a barbecue benefit for Make-A-Wish. I want to keep this goal as long as I'm alive. I got people to donate barbecue and pies, and I even got bands to come and play. The barbecue benefit is the one thing that's really helped me get a lot of bad things off my mind. I don't know how to put this in words. I just know I'm doing a good thing.

I Want to Help Kids

Charon, 18

When I get better, I want to help kids through their illnesses. I want to talk with them and make sure that they're not really down about it. I'll do just about anything to cheer them up. I want to see a smile on everyone's face! At the hospital, I try to do that whenever I'm there. My friend, Scott, has a cousin who's paralyzed. She goes around talking to people with disabilities. She just talks to them about life, and cheers them up. I was like, "That's the same thing I want to do!"

Helping a Mom

Blayne, 19

I had a physical therapist come to me and say, "We have a mom who's considering the baclofen pump for her child. Would you mind if we give you her phone number to talk to her and tell her about it?" I talked to this lady for two hours. She didn't know much about the pump. The doctors don't tell you everything. For example, you aren't going to be able to tie your shoes for three months because the pump is going to be in the way. I was very honest with the woman, which I hope she appreciated. Her child was too young to understand the decision that was being made. She opted not to do it, and frankly, I can't blame her. It's very invasive surgery and you have to be ready for it.

What's Really Important

Kimberlie, 10

I realize what is really important—being happy and nice to others. So many people have been so nice to me and my family. I can't even begin to name them all. People have held a rummage sale and sold lemonade to raise money for my treatments. I've received a puppy, lots of prayers, cards and gifts, a Make-A-Wish trip to Disney World, meeting the soccer star Tiffeny Milbrett, yummy dinners, and lots of hugs and comfort from my family and friends.

How do you ever thank all those people for being so nice to you? You help others. My family and I have tried really hard to make a difference. We've prayed for a lot of people and held fund-raisers for Pennies for Patients, The Relay for Life, and Make-A-Wish. We have sold bracelets for the Leukemia & Lymphoma Society, helped hurricane victims, and did a hat drive. We've also donated crafts, videos, games, and toys for kids in the hospital, and have done lots more things. It is really important to help others and to keep a positive attitude.

On the Speaking Tour
Justin, 12

I've made a lot of speeches to help raise money for cures. Our school did a Pennies for Patients drive and raised $2,000. I went around to several classrooms and gave a speech to raise money. I talked about my life and how I've struggled with cancer. I'd tell them what kind of cancers I've had, how I got through it, and what kinds of treatment I've had. I talked about how it's harder on girls to be bald than boys. When I speak, I have an outline prepared, but I always veer from it.

In my speeches I try to educate and help others. I tell them why we need to raise money and be more aware. I don't want other kids to have to go through what I've gone through. I try to use small words when I speak to younger classes, but you can't really use small words with cancer. They usually don't have any questions other than, "Did it hurt?" I said, "Yeah, it hurt pretty bad." Some of them asked me if I was going to die or if I were afraid I might die. I told them that there were times when I thought that way.

An Author and Renowned Speaker
Matthew, 9

I've coauthored two books with my mom. *My Brother Is Getting a New Port* was to help my younger brother when he was getting a new port. I had to get my port replaced when I was five, and I had a really tough time dealing with it. Then four weeks later, my little brother had to get his port replaced, too, and he was only two so he had no idea. I'm like "Oh, my gosh, my little brother is now going to have to go through this horrible thing." I was scared for him.

Rather than keeping me out of everything, my parents kept me involved, and I'm glad they did. My mom and I were talking about what my brother and I have gone through, and we decided to write a book to help other kids. It made me feel good to help other kids. We even gave tips, and most of the words describing things are ones I came up with.

Then we wrote *If You Wear a Medic Alert*. This started off by my mom asking me a bunch of questions and me answering them in my own words, so other kids could understand. We kind of role-played answering the questions and having fun to show there was nothing to be worried about. We tried to make things funny and accept-able. We wanted kids to know that it's not always easy talking about these things, and everyone has trouble talking about them.

My mom and I give talks about hemophilia. We did a presentation to my brother's kindergarten class last year. I think I helped a lot because I related to the kids, and they listened to me about the things I was explaining. My mom thinks I have a really good teaching style because the kids really understand things when I explain them. When she gives presentations at conferences around the country, I help out. I explain things from a kid's point of view, and that makes a difference to kids and to adults. Most of what I say I come up with on my own, but sometimes my mom helps me explain things. Sometimes she just interrupts me and I say, "Mom, I'm handling this just fine."

I Saved a Clinic

Blayne, 19

This one time I was working at a therapy horseback-riding clinic. It was one of the greatest experiences I've ever had because I could get on this horse and run. You have no idea what it means for me to be able to run. It's the coolest experience in the world. I could feel the horse's feet hit the ground. I was running! It was awesome!

Then the funding ran out for the program. I was 15 and I said to the lady who ran the place, "I know a lot of disabled people. If I can get you more clients, will you let me ride for free?" She said, "Do your best." I called the *Oregonian* newspaper and said, "You have this column on cool businesses that are doing things for the community. I work with a horseback-riding therapy facility that's doing great things. I'd like you to run a piece on them."

The reporter did this whole big, long piece on the facility, and it was on the front page of the "Life" section. We put in the article that there was going to be an open house and invited people to come. It was pouring rain the day of the open house, and we weren't expecting to see anyone.

But we had 15 people sign up that day!

Volunteer Work
Marian, 16

I volunteer for the Arthritis Foundation at the Children's Museum, and there are tons of kids there. My friends even came and worked with me there, and they now understand better about what I go through. When people don't see it firsthand, they don't get it as much. The other day, I baby-sat these girls who have arthritis. It was so nice to be able to help younger kids who are going through what I went through. My mom said, "Marian, you're a real role model to them just because they know you've been through it, too." A lot of them don't know if they're going to grow because they are on steroids. But when they see how normal I am, they know it's not that horrible. Being around other kids and helping others was really good for me.

Helping Kids Around the World
Matthew, 9

In America, kids with hemophilia can get factor and live normal lives. But in other countries, kids aren't as fortunate. Like in India, kids can have a bleed that won't stop and gangrene can set in. Then they have to have their limbs cut off. There was one boy in India who lost his leg because of a bleed in his big toe. In this country, if he had a bleed in his big toe and had factor, it would be nothing. But over there they can lose a whole leg.

My brother and I started a humanitarian group called JEM (Justin Erin Matthew) to help the kids in India and other places who don't have medical supplies. Any toy that we don't play with anymore, we send it to kids with hemophilia in other countries. We've sponsored a kid named Raj from India for three years. We did a garage sale one year and sent him the money from that.

Sickle Cell Fund-Raiser

Catyche, 20

My cousin, Daniel, and I held a fund-raiser to help raise money for my hospital, so the sickle cell kids can take field trips and have a support group. We invited several people, including doctors, to be speakers, and we had a dinner. I was there answering questions. My friend, Terri, also spoke. We did this thing where I asked Terri questions and she answered them so people would have an idea about what we go through. The whole event was a huge success. It created awareness and raised a lot of money.

Stopping the Bullying

Lindsey, 10

My family belongs to the Spina Bifida Association of America. The lady who is head of the association heard about this program to prevent bullying. They were looking for a disabled kid to be on the committee, and she suggested me. The meeting was in Washington, D.C., and my whole family went along. I loved it because we talked about how we could stop bullying in school. Sometimes kids will call me names like, "wheelie girl." Some kids in the halls will just stare at me. I think that's a way of bullying.

Last March, we launched the anti-bullying campaign in schools, including mine. We have an after-school program for kids whose parents work past the time school lets out. We were talking about taking kids on field trips for summer camp. Everyone was suggesting places to go. This little girl raised her hand and suggested going to a restaurant where they teach you how to make pasta. A fifth grader stood up and yelled, "No, you little twerp, you can't go there. That is a restaurant!" I was shocked. That's what I call bullying. She didn't realize that you can't take a bunch of kids into the kitchen of a restaurant. I felt really bad for her. Later, I went over and comforted her and told her about the campaign to prevent bullying. She went online and learned all about it. I felt really good because I actually helped her. Now she's not as scared as she was.

In Some Small Way

Amber, 15

When I was in the hospital, there was a little girl, Lindy, who had leukemia. Her mom said that I was like an older sister to her. I'd get on the floor and play with her and we'd laugh. We'd try to race, but since we were always hooked to things, like IVs, we couldn't do that too much. Lindy would come to my room a lot and knock on the door. There were days I wouldn't feel good, but I'd still let her come in and sit on the edge of my bed. Little kids don't understand what's going on. I'm sure they're thinking, "Why am I hooked to this big pole taller than me?" It would always make me feel better knowing that I was helping a little kid in the hospital, even when I was feeling bad. You feel like you're helping in some small way.

I'm Starting a Sickle Cell Support Group
Javlyn, 16

I have always wanted to help others understand what sickle cell is. My goal is to start a sickle cell support group. It's me and two other girls from the hospital who have sickle cell who are trying to start the group, along with mothers and friends of sickle cell patients. Our purpose is to get it out there and make people aware. We'll go to schools and talk to kids.

People think it's contagious. That's why when I talk about sickle cell, the first thing I say is, "You're born with it and it's not contagious." I don't want younger children with sickle cell to experience the cruelties that I did. I tell people, "Don't pick on those who are sick with anything. Don't pull away from that person. Try to be their friend and be there for support. Put yourself in their situation." Please help me to make the world aware of sickle cell.

A Little Hero
Autumn, 11

In the hospital, I became the "goodwill welcome wagon" for kids who were sad or angry, or who wouldn't come out of their rooms. A nurse would always come around when there was a new patient and say to me, "I've got someone I'd really like you to talk to." I'd go play with them or just tell them that things were going to be okay. Sometimes it took a while, but I always eventually got them to play with me, or talk, or come out of their rooms. I was a kid like them, and that always made them open up a little.

I liked doing that, it made me feel good to help others. Three years ago, right before I relapsed again, I won the "Littlest Hero" award for the state of North Carolina. We got to go to Disney for four days. That was awesome. I still don't know what I did to win, and I don't know who nominated me. It was probably because of what I did at the hospital.

I Wouldn't Change a Thing

Blayne, 19

I like to help people see me and themselves as more similar than different. I've been through all the emotional crap of a disabled person between the ages of zero and 19. My best friend in the whole world told me, "Blayne, before I met you, I thought, 'Oh, that poor guy,' and now I don't treat you any differently. You've just opened my eyes and I don't look at people the same way I used to."

I was able to help a lot of the kids at the camp I went to. There was an eight-year-old who had spina bifida. Not only was this kid homesick, but it had developed into, "Oh, why am I like this?" As a counselor, I was trained to deal with the homesickness, and as a person with a physical disability, I had just dealt with the same "why me" issue, so I had to handle this carefully.

I said to him, "The truth is we're better than people who aren't disabled. We know more and we've experienced more. They don't know what we know. We can help them. We have a great capacity for understanding and compassion and empathizing that comes along with being in our situations. You have to alter your situations around you to accommodate that."

I took him into the gym and we burned off some calories and some frustration by having a crawling race. We crawled back and forth until he was just exhausted. Then he asked me, "What do you mean we're better than them?" I said, "There's so much that you can learn from this experience, if you learn to accept it. But it doesn't have to happen today. You can be mad all you want." I told him that I was mad for years. I told him about all the experiences that I had, and that I was mad, too!

Another counselor at camp asked me where I got the passion for helping people. I explained that it had been a long, hard road and I didn't have anybody to go to. She said, "Okay, tell me the truth. Tell me the really crappy parts. Tell me this sucks!" I told her it does suck sometimes—that's the reality, but you can't make it your whole life.

But truth be told, today, if somebody came up to me and said we have a "pretty pill" that would make you forget all this crap and you'd be just like everybody else, I wouldn't take it. I am who I am because of what I've been through. People learn from experiences. And I can pass on what I've learned to others.

Super Cooper, the Therapy Dog
Sarah, 11

We're trying to get our dog, Cooper, certified to be a therapy dog so he can go into hospitals and help cheer up the kids. Bringing in a dog will make them feel better because that happened to me. When I was in the hospital, I loved the therapy dogs. I'll be able to talk to kids about my dog and get their minds off other things.

To get certified, there's this big test the dogs have to go through. You have to drop a pan in front of your dog to see if it reacts crazy to the loud noise. Then they make you go into a different room for three minutes, and your dog has to stay and know how to sit. I think Cooper can handle it. A dog can't get certified until it's a year old, so I'm training Cooper for when he's old enough to test.

When I Get Better, I'm Going to Help Other Kids
Hope, 12

It's amazing how many kids are admitted for chemo and their families just drop them off and come back in a week. Most of the time, their parents have to work extra jobs and also take care of their other kids. I feel really bad for them. When I get better, my sister and I are going to go back and visit the kids at the hospital who don't have people sitting with them, just to keep them positive. They need to know that someone is there with them. I think it would be good to help decorate other kids' rooms with happy things, like people always decorated mine. You just have to do everything you can, always.

Hair and Patients
Elyse, 13

Recently I visited Sophie, a friend of our family. She's nine and has broken bones and a head injury from a skiing accident. I made her laugh, which she needed, and I was an encouragement to her. My advice to her was don't eat the bran muffins in the hospital. The cheese omelets are good, and the root beer floats are good. It was great to see her laugh. Because she wasn't back in school yet, it was encouraging to her to know that I was back in school and it was going great. I just told her how things might be, and to not get down because everything was going to be okay. I told her to call me if she needed to talk.

Wheelchair Accessible Planning
Jonathan, 21

I helped eliminate structural barriers and improve access for wheelchairs where I lived, and I was the youngest member of my city's planning board.

Passionate About Helping
Blayne, 19

I love horses. Horses are one of the most amazing, calming animals in the world. I would almost go as far as to say there is a psychic connection. Just touching a horse is therapeutic to kids with disabilities. I volunteer at the stables a lot taking care of the horses and helping the kids. Also, for a couple of years I have been spending one day a week at a kindergarten reading to kids.

I live with a single mother who has two kids, a four-year-old and a 13-year-old. I have been able to help out the older son in some of his emotional issues. He's acting out all over the place, and I can help him because I've been there, too. I have been able to take some of the stress off of his mom. It's been a really good coupling of strengths and weaknesses because, truth be told, I can't do everything. You are not going to find me mopping a floor, but if you clean my house, I'll tend to your kids.

Sharing the Wealth
Hope, 12

Every time I was in the hospital, I got special attention from the nurses. One time, this nurse came in and told us that she had meal tickets we could use in the cafeteria to eat for free. Since I was already suspicious about the extra stuff we always got, I asked her, "Does everyone get these meal tickets?" She said, "No." I said, "Okay. We'll take as many as you'll give us." She gave us a bunch of meal tickets. I immediately ordered my mother to take all of the meal tickets to the break room and give them to all the people who really needed them. We weren't rich, but we had enough money to pay for our own food. I could tell that there were people there who really needed those meal tickets.

Pennies for Patients
Sarah, 11

Pennies for Patients was a program at schools to raise money for the Cancer Society. I was the honorary person for the schools. The day I came to visit a school, they had "bandana day." All the kids wore bandanas like mine. I didn't have any hair at that time. It was really neat to see 100 kids wearing bandanas. The school raised $5,000 in about a month.

I really try to give back as much as possible. I've done TV interviews and commercials to help spread the word and help others. We did a radio commercial and newspaper ad for the hospital after the first time I relapsed. I've also worked with the Children's Miracle Network on TV to raise money.

My Diary Is to Help
Aaron, 15

I have a diary where I have written about everything since I got diagnosed with cancer. I want to publish my diary and have the profits go to cancer organizations. When people read it, they will know what I've been through and know that somebody else has been through what they are experiencing. Knowing that makes things better sometimes.

Life's a Party
Miriam, 19

I want to go back and help sick kids, because when I was sick in the hospital, I couldn't find anybody to talk to. I want to be able to give them positive reinforcement. Attitude is extremely important when you have an illness like cancer. That's why I was able to leave the hospital a month earlier than the doctors told me I would. I set my mind to it. I was like, "I can't have a negative attitude because I'll never get better."

Life's a party. You have to live it up. That's why I get mad at people who worry about me. I get mad at people who worry over the minimal things. My parents and brother really sacrificed for me when I was sick. With my job, I give my parents money so they can get further along on their bills. I'd rather be broke than see them worry about money. I'll get by. I help my brother a lot too. He calls me his second mom, and for Mother's Day, he even got me a present.

Helping My Aunt Deal

Nadia, 12

I had been on dialysis for years when my aunt found out that she had to go on dialysis. She was very nervous about it. I told her that she didn't have to be scared, and that she was going to be okay, because I'm already going through it and I'm okay.

I Helped My Friend Deal

Blayne, 19

I have a friend who's going through Bell's palsy. She woke up one morning and her entire face was paralyzed. She called me, horribly depressed, slurring her speech and looking for inspiration. I gave her everything I had, and it felt great! She told me that she had people give her all kinds of advice on how to handle things. I said, "You know, you're going to be able to do that for other people."

She Just Wanted to Donate Money

Justin, 12

I make colorful lizards from plastic beads, and I sell them. Many of them are used as key rings. At one of the many fund-raising auctions we did outside the hospital to raise money for my stem cell surgery, one of my lizards sold for $3,200. There was a bidding war with my aunt, who really wanted the lizard, but she couldn't afford to pay that much. Finally, she just gave up and a woman bought the lizard for the $3,200. We had never met her before. Then she gave my aunt the beaded lizard. It was so cool—the woman basically just donated $3,200. My aunt had me make another beaded lizard just like it, and she mailed it to the generous woman.

Chapter 11

Advice and Wisdom—Never Give Up

"**Keeping a good attitude** and keeping busy so you don't think about things are the most important things to **keep you going.**" —José

"**Cancer isn't my life, and I do everything in my power** to not make it my life." —Aaron

"I'm not worried if my cancer comes back. If it comes back, it comes back. If it doesn't, yippee. I only see the **opportunity to fight it.**" —Miriam

Here's our insight and encouragement for kids like us, and for kids not like us. We've been through a lot and learned a lot, the hard way. Here's how we cope with things that most other kids our age don't even have to think about. We have some ideas about what really matters in life that could help you deal with the problems you face. We hope you can learn from us, to find your way.

Fight to Your Last Breath
Amber, 15

You gotta keep fighting to your last breath, no matter what, and remember people are pulling for you. Be a real fighter, and have the best attitude you can. Don't give up. At first, I didn't want to fight. I just wanted to lie down and do nothing because I was so sick and depressed. When we came home after the third chemo treatment, I'd just lie on the couch—wouldn't eat, wouldn't drink, wouldn't talk. My parents got so mad. They said, "You cannot stop fighting! If you do, we're losing this battle today." Now I say, "Even though I'm still battling it, why did I ever want to give up?"

> "I'm not afraid of anything. I have a strong will to live."
> —*Tonya*

Patience
Marian, 16

If you have an illness, be patient and keep working hard and learn to accept what you have, instead of fighting against it. Work with it—not to use it to take advantage of situations, but to accept it, and learn how to live with it.

Be There for Your Friend
Javlyn, 16

If you have friends in need, don't pull away. Try to be there for them. Treat them the same as always; be sympathetic, try to understand, and be supportive. Ask if there's some way you could help. Most of the time, they just need a friend. The best way is to try to put yourself in their situation. Comfort them and tell them to do the best they can to stay healthy. Go to your friend's house and just be with them. Encourage them to fight and take their medicine.

You have to go on and keep living your life the best you can. When I get depressed, I do something fun like be with my friends and family, or go to the mall or movies. I would tell other kids who get depressed to do something they like to get their mind off of it. You need support from friends and other people in your life.

Advice to Die For

Faith, 20

My social worker told me that I should write a will to describe where I want to be buried, and how I want to die. She said if I wasn't going to take my medicine, I would end up dying. That scared me. I didn't write up a will or anything. I just told my sister about how I wanted things to be, like where to be buried and stuff. And I started taking my medicine again. I don't want to die this young. I know I have to do what they tell me. It's hard because you just get tired of doing it every day, but you've got to do it so you can live. Life is a precious gift.

Stop Worrying, Treat Me Normal, and Check Out My Web Site

Hope, 12

When people find out what I have, they always freak out. They always treat me different, which I hate! They always ask, "How is your cancer?" like that's the only thing there is about me anymore. They never want to talk about anything normal, only my cancer and asking me if I'm going to die. That really makes me angry. I just want people to treat me normal. The only thing that's keeping me from doing exactly everything they do is my crutches.

People just weren't being themselves around me. I got sick of telling the same story over and over again, so I got a Web site through a place called Caring Bridge to update people on my condition. It's great having the Web site because it's the truth and doesn't turn out to be some stretched story, like what often happens when news travels from person to pereson. When I first got my Web site, my mom and dad were writing on it when I wasn't feeling up to it or didn't have anything to write. But they were telling people my deep, dark secrets! My mom would tell all these things, I mean like everything. I'd say, "You didn't tell *that*?" I cut them off, and they lost their Web site writing privilege.

I Turned Out a Regular Kid

Nadia, 12

The first thing I'd tell kids is that I really want to be like everyone else. Treat me the same. The only thing that's different is dialysis. I play at recess like everyone else, except I just can't be hit in the stomach. I'd also tell kids to be grateful for the kidneys they have and, if they ever get what I got, don't worry because you just have to do dialysis and that will keep you alive and healthy. I turned out a regular kid.

Don't Stop Being the Same
Brittney, 15

Don't stop being who you are just because you're sick. You still can do the things that you love, even though it might take more effort or more time. Don't ever give up! Fight to win because you never know what could happen in life. If you have a friend who gets cancer, don't abandon her because that would make her feel like she did something wrong or like an outcast.

Laugh!
Miriam, 19

Always laugh—that's one thing my mom taught me. Laugh at the situation and make it fun. Make fun of your doctors and nurses and every person you see, 'cause at the end you're gonna leave laughing. To feel better, I go shopping. I'm a girl—what can I say?

The Standard Advice
Elyse, 13

My advice is what people have told me one thousand million times, "You just have to keep on trying." If you're tired of hearing that, my advice is to bite the doctor. If you bite the doctor, you'll feel better—and he might stay away for a while.

Friends Are Everything
Sarah, 11

If you have friends who are sick like me, spend a lot of time with them because they might not have many people around them. One of my friends came and played with me, even if I was in the hospital just for one day. It really made a difference to me.

Don't Look Things Up on the Internet
Catyche, 20

When I was 15, I researched my illness on the Internet. I got so upset! I read that you can go blind, you can get scoliosis, and that you're gonna die at age 20. I was like, "Oh, my God! This is horrible!" That's what made me decide not to research any more on the Internet. I told my doctor about it, and he said you have to be careful about what you read because it can be exaggerated or even be totally wrong. Anyone can post things on the Internet, and it's not always people who have experience with that disease, or who are doctors. Don't look up your disease on the Internet and go scaring yourself.

Sometimes, Even the Doctors Just Don't Know
Alan, 20

The doctors did not think that I would come out of my long coma with such good results. Also, they are surprised that I continue to progress and have not reached a plateau in my recovery. Even though they were surprised and cautiously optimistic, they always encouraged me. They watched with amazement, as did I, at the things I was increasingly able to do. For example, no one thought I would be able to walk across the stage at my high school graduation. But I did it, with the help of a walker. I'm continuing to improve at everything. You just have to keep moving forward.

The Guy in the Glass
Blayne, 19

I've kept a journal since I was eight years old about everything I have gone through. A lot of the teenage stuff is really interesting. I've got binders full of thoughts, ideas, and favorite poems. I have a favorite poem of mine that I memorized when I was 12 that totally fits my situation. It's called "The Guy in the Glass," by Dale Wimbrow. It makes the point that no matter who you are, what you are going through, or what anyone else thinks, the only person who really matters is that person in the mirror. I encourage everyone to find this poem and read it.

Truth be told, I spent so much time trying to appease other people and convince them that I wasn't any different, that I really didn't tell myself that it was okay for me to be me. Even after memorizing that poem, I still didn't get it. About three years ago, I hit my lowest point and said, "What's the point in any of this?" I read the poem to my friend, Sue, the social worker at the hospital. She's the greatest woman I've ever met, and she's done wonders for me. When I read the poem, she said, "You know, Blayne, you need to take your own advice. You're the only one who matters. Quit thinking about what other people think, and proving to them that you're smart and capable. You have only to prove it to yourself." It finally clicked for me.

> "We're all just different in different ways, that's all."
> —Jonathan

Don't Go Giving Us Big Shoves
Lindsey, 10

I'll be pushing myself around the track at school, and people will walk up behind me and think they are helping me by giving me a big shove. It really slows me down and throws me off my pace. I don't like it. I try to do everything by myself. So when you see me, or kids like me, going at our own pace, don't go giving us big shoves. Sometimes your "help" actually slows us down.

Don't Be Afraid—Strategize
Miriam, 19

Don't be afraid of cancer. It's not the "boogie man." The "boogie man" is a figment of our imagination. Cancer is a reality. Any type of illness is a reality—a reality check for ourselves and our families. When it hits home, it makes you think. After you're done thinking, you have to strategize. First, you definitely need to go in the positive direction—that everything's gonna go well and you're gonna win.

Then there's, "What if I die?" Right before my stem cell operation, my doctors told me, "Okay, Miriam, here's the deal. The chemotherapy is going to give you heart failure, lung failure, liver failure, kidney failure, and brain damage. All in all, you might die. What do you want to do?" I was like, "Let's do it. I'm not going down without a fight!"

I wasn't scared. Dying is something that happens when it happens. I could have died when I had a 108 fever. My coworkers say the 108 fever has probably made me lose brain cells. They make fun of me because they love me . . . I think.

One Doctor

Meredith, 10

One doctor told my mom that I'd never walk again. My mom got mad at him. You just can't always listen to the doctors. I do walk, with help. They don't know everything.

No Big Deal

Justin, 6

I would tell kids with hemophilia to not be upset about it. We can do everything other kids get to do. If I saw a kid with a port, I would say, "How do you like having a port?" It would be a great icebreaker.

Get Up and Go

Jonathan, 21

I don't care what your "deal" is, go and enjoy life! It's very easy to get down and be mad at the world and take your anger out on people. If there's an area that you need to work on to make it better for you and others, do it. Think positive and know that you are important and can make a difference in life, regardless of your so-called limitations. Do your best to make a difference.

Don't Panic

Hope, 12

If you have cancer, don't panic. Stay strong—some cancer can be cured. It doesn't mean you're going to die. Don't let yourself get down. I almost did that. I would just sit in my hospital bed and wouldn't talk. I'd tell kids to do all the positive things, like watch a movie and try to get out of your hospital bed and sit up in the chair even if you don't feel like it. I did that and I felt better. The best thing you can have, no matter what, is a positive attitude.

Being Blind Is Only Temporary

Cassidy, 7

I'd tell blind kids, "Guys, it's okay. You're just going to be blind for a while." I'm not going to be blind forever, only until I'm in heaven. It's okay. I do things like every other kid, like write music and play golf. I'd tell kids who aren't blind to not make fun of kids who are blind or don't have noses, like me. It hurts our feelings.

Believe in Yourself

Autumn, 11

To be more confident, believe in yourself. Try to be high-spirited and don't worry about what other people think. Focus on yourself. Don't try to be what other people want you to be.

Letting It All Go

Charon, 18

I never thought about how it would be with only one leg until after the surgery. I started thinking about how people would look at me. How were girls gonna look at me? How are my brothers and sisters gonna look at me? In the hospital, I always closed my door and stayed in the room. I was in my room for two days straight thinking about all of this. That's when I decided to let it all go because I had to deal with it. My leg would be gone for the rest of my life, and people were gonna look at me the way they chose. I couldn't change that. I decided I wasn't gonna be depressed for the rest of my life. I just threw it all away. I was still me, and I was gonna still do what I wanted to do.

Walk in My Shoes

Jonathan, 21

I hear people complain about the least little thing, like getting their hair wet from the rain. That always makes me upset, people complaining about those little things. Be thankful for what you have because it could be a whole lot worse. Believe me, I know. There's always someone else who's worse off than you.

Take Control
Miriam, 19

Take control of the situation. It's your life. Make things work for you—don't make things work against you.

> "The best thing you can have, no matter what, is a positive attitude." —Hope

How Can I Help YOU?
Blayne, 19

I have bladder issues, and I would sometimes lose control. Kids especially are vicious when they pick on you. They had no idea that I wet my pants because I'm disabled and can't control my bladder. I had a great teacher in fourth grade who told me, "Blayne, this little piece of advice will serve you well: People who pick on you have problems with themselves."

Even as an adult, I get picked on. Now I look at it like, "Okay, how can I help *you*? How can I make *you* feel better about yourself because *you* have to be mean to me to make yourself feel better." Being able to tell someone that just blows them away.

It's All About How You Handle Things
Luke, 22

Attitude is a huge part of getting through anything. No matter what the situation, I think it makes a huge difference if you deal with everything with a sense of humor. That seems to make it a lot easier. It did for me. When I had bad days or was feeling depressed, I'd try to stay away from people so I wasn't mean to anybody. I'd kinda pull myself away from everything and everybody so I could get over it and feel fine.

Very Personal, but Very Important
Mason, 16

The day before chemo, we asked the doctor if I should go to the sperm bank, in case the cancer or chemo might make me sterile. I had read about this in Lance Armstrong's book, *It's Not About the Bike*. Since he had testicular cancer, it was one of the options he chose. The doctor said it was probably a good idea. It has more to do with the chemo than the cancer. Chemo kills off everything, all of the cells—the good, the bad, and the ugly. I was 15 at the time. I didn't really wanna bring it up to the doctor. It was a little sensitive. My dad talked to the doctor, and I'm glad he did.

You need to bring up embarrassing or sensitive topics because you never know. The doctors didn't mention that I could become sterile. Most people never think about it, and then it's too late. I told my friends about it. It wasn't a big deal to me. They thought it was funny. They made jokes, ones you can probably imagine and that I can't repeat.

Not the End of the World
Lindsey, 10

We had this dance class where they help kids with cerebral palsy stretch their arms. The teacher for the class had just gone snow skiing, and she fell and broke her leg. She was in a wheelchair. I actually taught her how to use her wheelchair. At the end of dance class, we would go zooming down the ramp together, and she was glad that she broke her leg because of the fun we had. My basketball coach walked until he was a teenager, then he ran into a tree while skiing and was paralyzed.

It's okay to be in a wheelchair. It's not the end of the world. I'd try to get kids happy with the way they are because it's not actually a bad thing. Being in a wheelchair is just part of life, especially if you know that there's probably nothing that you can do about it. Don't be embarrassed—be secure with who you are. The wheelchair is not your enemy. It's like an assistant for you.

The first time I got into a wheelchair I was like, "Okay, what do I do with it?" I would just sit there. Then I realized that if I didn't use my wheelchair, I wasn't going to get anywhere. I realized that being in a wheelchair was better than being stuck in one spot all the time. Be glad that you're alive, and that you have the wheelchair to help you.

I Knew I'd Be Fine—No Doubt
Mason, 16

I didn't just wish and think and hope that I'd be okay—I *knew* I was going to be okay. It really is attitude that makes a big difference. I think even my parents and brother were helped by my attitude. If you have a good attitude, then they know you are going to be fine. So keep a positive attitude. Never think about the bad things that could happen.

Always think that everything's gonna be all right. Because you never know. We don't have to always think the worst. Things have as much of a chance of getting better as they do getting worse. Keep telling yourself that you're going to be fine.

Learn from Me
José, 11

To feel better, the first thing I do after treatments is go to sleep and try to relax. Then when I wake up, I eat and play with my electronic games. I try not to think about the treatments and all that stuff. If you do, you just get depressed because there is nothing happy about it. Okay, sometimes I scream and throw things. When I'm too much that way, my mom gives me medicine that helps me sleep. Sometimes I get angry at my mom because she's there with me all the time. In the hospital she stays with me every day, all day. I guess that's kinda natural, when you're sick for days on end—you get mad at the person closest to you, who is there all the time with you. I just want to say to my mom that I'm sorry. She knows I didn't mean anything but, you know . . .

If You Suddenly Go Bald
Hope, 12

If you ever suddenly go bald for some reason, just sit under a fan. It feels so good. To feel the air on your head without hair feels so incredibly good. Not too many people can do that, especially kids.

Celebrate Your Differences
Blayne, 19

Don't treat us any different, but be aware that we are different. Instead of analyzing those differences, celebrate them. I think that's the biggest key to dealing with anything you don't understand. Instead of focusing on the differences and saying, "That kid walks funny," or "That kid whatever . . . ," celebrate those differences. Because, truth be told, if you listen to someone who is different, and you hear what they have to say, you're going to learn something. Just like if I listen to you and hear what you have to say, I'm going to learn something.

You're Not Alone
Aaron, 15

If you are sick with anything, don't forget you're never, ever alone. Never! It's not something that you have to go through by yourself. Everybody is there for you. If you don't have family with you every moment in the hospital, there are always people, like the wonderful nurses, who make you feel so much better every day. My mom works about 12 hours a day. She can't stay the nights because she has to get up and go to work. I wouldn't see her again until 7:00 at night in the hospital. But that didn't stop my day. My nurse, Trish, would spend hours with me, even when she wasn't supposed to. You always have help, and miracles happen every day.

Be Careful What You Tell Kids
Blayne, 19

I was sitting on the couch, I was probably five. My aunt was on one side and my mother was on the other. We were watching a movie completely unrelated to being handicapped, and I just started bawling. They're like, "What's the matter?" I'm like, "Why am I like this? Why is nobody else like this? Why do I have to be the only one?" They gave me the answer that ruined things for me for years. They said, "Because God chose you special." I took that as, "Well, then damn you, God! Why would you do that, you big jerk?" For years, that's how I felt. I know they said it to try and make me feel special, but it just really pissed me off. I'm sure they never thought it would backfire into making me hate God for years. I never told my family that. I just took it as, "Well, God had this thing out for me."

Learn to See the Best Side of . . . Whatever
Cassidy, 7

You need to learn to see the good side of everything. For example, because I'm blind, I hear better than everyone else. I hear the ice cream truck two neighborhoods away. No one else can hear it! On the nature trail, I hear snakes when no one else hears a thing. I can hear the sounds when they put the dam up and let the water flow, and the dam is five miles away. Also, no one can ever sneak up on me, I hear too well!

Passing Time with the MRI
Abbie, 13

Having an MRI takes a long time, and you have to lie there still. A good tip for kids who have to go through an MRI is to make up songs. The MRI makes clicking sounds, and I make up music to go along with it to pass the time.

I Recommend Meditation
Mason, 16

After chemo treatments and my surgery, I meditated and made sure that every single part of my body was cancer-free, and that the cancer wouldn't come back. I concentrated on breathing in clean, clear air that would go through my body and breathe out the bad. It also helped me to relax. It was great. I knew I would be fine, but meditating made me feel calm and receptive to healing—good, positive energy. When you take deep breaths, visualize the bad cells leaving. It's good to have that tool because it's always with you. It can do no harm. It's not a voodoo-hoodoo thing because, obviously, I believed in the medicine, too.

This Works!
Hope, 12

If you get sick and tired of having to answer questions about your illness, do what I do. Since I've gone to the doctor and learned all these new words, whenever my friends pester me about how things are going, I start using words like "methotrexate" and "cisplatin." They're like, "What?" That always shuts them up!

Don't Forget the Siblings!
Kimberlie, 10

I think it is really nice when people bring gifts for, or give special attention to, the siblings of the kid who is sick. Sometimes brothers and sisters feel left out, and it's hard on them in their own way—they need cheering up, too! I knew those gifts and attention meant a lot to my sister, and helped her deal with some things.

Cancer Made Me Better
Charon, 18

I had a lot of friends say, "Man, you're lucky. You get to lie in bed and watch TV all day, and get gifts." I was like, "Trust me, you wouldn't like lying in bed all day watching TV. Every place I went, and everything I had gotten, I would give all of that stuff back to have my leg." I'd love to walk again with my real leg and play football. But then I stop thinking about that, and I look at the good stuff that came out of it. I met new friends. If I hadn't been in the hospital, I wouldn't have met Mason and his family.

Cancer has changed my life for the better. If this hadn't happened to me, I wouldn't be so focused. Before, I didn't have goals. I didn't care about school. I was heading down the road to being a dropout. Now, I'm really trying to make it, and trying to go to college. Before, nobody was helping me. Now, there are a lot of people helping me get where I need to be. I have a lot of people believing in me, because they see that I believe in me now.

I have a lot of people looking up to me saying, "You are strong. I don't know anyone with one leg who's happy like you, and always has a smile on his face." I'm not happy about everything, but I'm happy about most things.

I Found Myself in the Most Beautiful Way
Miriam, 19

The best thing about going through all this cancer and treatments is that I found myself. A lot of people, especially teenagers, don't have the opportunity to find themselves. They find themselves later on in life. That's why they go to school for 10 years and don't know what they want to be. They do things without being conscious of it because they're insecure about themselves. I have my insecurities, and I know what they are. I have my strong points, and I know what they are. I found myself in the most beautiful way. I matured in the coolest way.

Don't Get Hung Up on Words
Blayne, 19

Socially acceptable words change often. I use the word "gimp" when I'm describing myself. I know it is totally derogatory, but I like to have fun with words. I call the handicapped transportation service the "Gimp Mobile." I use the word "handicapped" because that's what my parents used. "Physically challenged" just seems like way too much work. I don't like "disabled" because "dis" means "not," so disabled means "not abled." I am abled.

I Will Run Again
Mason, 16

I want to run again. That's one of my goals. Every day, I strengthen my right leg as much as I can. Even when walking upstairs, I make sure to use my right leg and not cheat. I work out in PE at school every day for forty-five minutes. I do leg presses. We took the school's PE program to my physical therapist to make sure things I shouldn't do would be eliminated and replaced by other things that are beneficial. Also, I stayed on the varsity baseball team last season. Between chemo treatments, I would dress for games whenever I could. Some of my teammates would rub my bald head for luck when they went up to bat. I used to play first base, but now I pitch.

Motivating Factors
Marian, 16

My medical condition has changed me. I think I'm more sympathetic toward people who are sick because I can sympathize with them and understand them more than most people. I don't know how to explain it. It just seems that I have to work harder than most people to get through the days, and I think that's strengthened me. It's motivated me to do better, too—to succeed more. People get upset when they have the flu or something, and they overdramatize it. I'm like, "That's nothing."

There Are Good Things About Having Cancer
Aaron, 15

You see things differently and appreciate things a lot more when you have cancer. You don't take things for granted anymore. You appreciate how much people appreciate you, and how much you're needed. You change a lot.

I Am Sooo Not Pitiful

Blayne, 19

You need to take your experiences and run with them. You are only bound by what you think you can't do. You can do anything you want to do—anything in the world. Whatever "it" is, you find ways around it, you find ways over it, and you find ways through it. You will get through it and to the other side.

It's not a given that you go through an experience and learn from it. You have to reflect on that experience and say, "What can I learn from it?" What happens most often is that people go through a horrible experience and have a "poor pitiful me" attitude, and think the whole experience sucked. It does suck! But you take from it, and you learn from it. I wouldn't give up any of my experiences for anything. How many kids can say that?

Epilogue

It has taken four years to complete all the interviews, so here are the cool (and tragic) things that have happened to us since we were interviewed. Our voices live on.

Justin (with hemophilia)

Justin continues to do wonderfully. He still swims, plays the piano, and lives a normal young boy's life. Justin and his brother, Matthew, still maintain their humanitarian group called JEM (Justin Erin Matthew) to help the kids in India and other places who don't have medical supplies.

Cassidy

Cassidy attends the Governor Morehead School for the Blind, which has enhanced programs for the visually impaired, including cooking, laundry, and grocery shopping. Cassidy takes Tae Kwon Do, plays softball and the piano, and is learning to play guitar and cello. She still wants to become a talk show host. She has started her multiple surgeries to build her a nose.

Matthew

Matthew is doing great, and he still writes books and gives speeches with his mother. He plays sports and the piano. Matthew and his brother, Justin, still maintain their humanitarian group called JEM (Justin Erin Matthew) to help the kids in India and other places who don't have medical supplies.

Kimberlie

Kimberlie works to make a difference and give back, including fundraising for Make-A-Wish, The Leukemia & Lymphoma Society, and Relay for Life. She plays soccer, basketball, volleyball, and tennis, and concentrates her energy on living life to the fullest, spending time with her friends, and attending school instead of being in the hospital.

Lindsey

Lindsey plays wheelchair basketball and competes in track and field. She holds a national record in archery from the Junior National Disability Championships. She water skis, snow skis, and rides horseback at the Misty Meadows Mitey Riders therapeutic riding academy. Her goal is to participate in the Paralympics.

Meredith

Meredith uses her crutches at home, but uses a motorized wheelchair at school and at the mall. She maintains excellent grades and recently finished third in the nation in the Daughters of the American Revolution essay contest. She is a member of the Whiteville High Juniorettes (a service organization) and the National Forensic League debate and public speaking team.

Autumn

Autumn recently had a scare that the cancer had returned; during the subsequent operation, she crashed and had to be revived. It wasn't cancer but rather a cyst on her ovary, and they removed her final ovary. She had seven subsequent surgeries, but she is five years into remission and lives her life to the fullest.

Ivy

Ivy is cancer-free, but the cancer impacted her motor and speech skills. She is improving in both areas, but it's doubtful that she will ever be able to walk by herself. When her classmates avoided or tormented her, Ivy's mother went to school and spoke with them to help them understand and be more accepting of Ivy. Today, Ivy has lots of friends at school and continues to do well.

José

José's cancer worsened. He began experimental drug therapy but that did not help, and he passed away. To the end, he remained strong with a positive attitude. His family and friends miss him dearly.

Sarah

Sarah is in remission and doing very well. She receives straight A's and is on her school's swim team. She won the Scholastic Gold Art Award and had her art, a crayon etching titled "Summer Afternoon," displayed in a Washington, D.C., art gallery. Sarah volunteers at a pediatric oncology clinic. Unfortunately, Cooper, her dog she was training to become a therapy dog, didn't make the cut—something about his temperament.

Scotty

Scotty's condition remains about the same. He uses his wheelchair to get around and has started lifting weighs to strengthen his arms.

Mookie

Mookie had to undergo increased amounts of chemo, which put her into ICU for several days. The chemo worked and Mookie is in remission. Her diabetes is under control due to her diet and insulin shots. She is living as a normal teen and has returned to competitive sports. She's taking classes for a crime scene investigation career.

Hope

Hope lost her battle with cancer and passed away. Because of her unselfish wish to grant the wishes of other kids, Make-A-Wish dedicated its 2004 Annual Report to Hope; Claire's Boutiques sold over 200,000 Handbags of Hope with Hope's story attached; and Hope was featured in *Reader's Digest* magazine.

Jessica

Jessica is doing very well, although she had to adjust how she does some things. Her treatments caused a condition called AVN (decreased blood flow in her bones, causing cells to die) in her ankles, knees, and wrists. She had surgery in both knees to remedy the condition and is doing better, but she can no longer play sports, which disappoints her.

Justin (with cancer)

Justin had an infection that went undiagnosed for months, causing him to miss school. With heavy antibiotics he recovered fully and is doing great. He enjoys sports, games, his friends, and cooking—he wants to become a chef. He speaks about cancer, volunteers in the hospital, and does fund-raising, expanding from making beaded lizards to making beautiful beaded bracelets.

Nadia

Nadia received a kidney transplant, donated by her father. She had complications related to the transplant, which kept her in the hospital for months. She is doing better, but still has some diet restrictions. She volunteers at a childcare center and attends school full time. She goes to kidney camp each year and is becoming a camp counselor.

Abbie

Abbie is cancer-free but her coordination has been affected, limiting her play in competitive sports. She has occasional bouts of clumsiness and "drop foot," and some short-term memory loss. Her spirits remain high as she leads an active life with many friends and gets great grades in school. She volunteers at church and school, and participates in a program researching kids who have brain cancer.

Elyse

Elyse attends school full time. She made great improvements in walking long distances to important places like the local pizza and smoothie shops. She exercises to strengthen herself, enjoys drama classes, and wants to become a novelist.

Aaron

Aaron's bone marrow transplant failed and she passed away. She maintained a positive attitude to the end. She is greatly missed by her family and friends.

Amber

Amber lost her fight with cancer. To her final days, she sought to continue Hope's wish of helping other kids get their wishes. After her passing, her family and friends had her birthday party to celebrate her life, as she had asked. Her family set up a scholarship in Amber's name.

Brittney

Brittney had four more bouts of different types of cancer and is undergoing treatment. She had multiple surgeries. Her younger brother, Jordan, was diagnosed with cancer. Brittney looks forward to college where she'll major in writing. She wants to travel the world and live in New Zealand. She lives by the motto: "Obstacles are put in your way to see if what you want is really worth fighting for."

Javlyn

Javlyn deals with pain from her sickle cell crises, but still maintains a positive attitude. She strives to live her life as a "normal" teen. She still works very hard to educate people about sickle cell anemia and is involved with her sickle cell support group, which she founded.

Marian

Marian contracted mononucleosis, which threw her into a rare complication of her systemic juvenile rheumatoid arthritis called macrophage activation syndrome. She fought for her life in ICU on a ventilator for nine days. She has since made a complete recovery, although the crisis left her with some residual lung damage. She plans to attend Vanderbilt University.

Mason

Mason is cancer-free, but struggles with the mechanics of his surgical leg implants. He rode with Lance Armstrong as the Ride for the Roses Guest Survivor in Austin, Texas. Mason is in college and wants to become a pediatric oncologist. His father, Scott, founded drumSTRONG, an annual event that raises funds, awareness, and support for local and national cancer initiatives.

Charon

Charon attended his senior prom but passed away the day before his high school graduation ceremony. His friend, Mason, accepted his diploma on his behalf. After his diagnosis, Charon rededicated himself to his education and to serving others, and wanted to make a career helping counsel young people through adverse health and socioeconomic challenges.

Ryan

Ryan graduated from high school, a third-year art honor student. He decided art was not for him, and is an entrepreneur with his mother in their business that loads tunes, videos, movies, podcasts, educational lectures, and audio textbooks onto MP3 players. He drives a car with hand controls and spends time with his friends.

Blayne

Blayne still struggles to walk. He is not as mobile as he used to be due to the increased pain from the pressure on his legs because he no longer uses crutches, and he has had to get a wheelchair. He goes through bouts of depression but is thankful for his wonderful mind. He's in college to become a therapist in the mental health field.

Miriam

Miriam is healthy and in remission. She's in college, majoring in marketing and management. She works two jobs to pay for college and contribute to her family's living expenses.

Alan

Alan's speech is improving. He uses his Lightwriter for school and when he has a lot to say. He walks with a walker, although he struggles with his balance. He rides horses for therapy, and can sit up straight in the saddle. He is in his third year at college, majoring in literature, and he works out at a gym three times a week.

Catyche

Catyche's condition worsened and she suffered serious seizures, acute sickle cell crises, and blood clots. She spent months in the hospital. Her medical condition has since improved dramatically. She no longer uses a wheelchair, uses oxygen only at night, and is able to go weeks without any pain. She is now able to attend college on campus.

Faith

Faith continues with her medications and remains healthy while living with HIV. She lost weight and works out regularly to maintain her health. She has her own apartment and works in a childcare center.

Jonathan

Jonathan's family built a new, accessible home for him. He picked out the light fixtures, plumbing, carpet, kitchen decor, and wall colors. He passed away one week before the house was completed. His family misses him dearly and established a scholarship in his name.

Luke

Luke had oddities in his blood. The doctors attributed it to his spleen, and removed it. That fixed the problem, but he developed ITP (low blood platelets), making him more prone to bruising and bleeding. In a recent scan, doctors detected something suspicious on his lymph nodes. He'll have a biopsy after the doctors can stabilize his blood platelets. He began school to become a motorcycle mechanic.

Glossary of Medical Terms

We have all learned a lot of new words through our experiences—words you usually don't hear in "normal" kid talk. Here's where we define these words in terms kids can understand.

Acute respiratory distress syndrome (ARDS): a life-threatening lung failure that occurs when lungs fill with fluid and collapse.

Arthritis: inflammation or stiffness of the joints. There are three basic types of arthritis:

- pauciarticular: this type generally affects four or fewer joints, usually the knees, elbows, wrist, and ankles.

- polyarticular: this type affects more than four joints, usually the small joints of the hands as well as the knees, ankles, hips, and feet.

- systemic onset (also called Still's disease): this type affects many body systems and is accompanied by fever and chills and sometimes a rash on the thighs and chest. A child may also experience enlargement of the spleen and lymph nodes; inflammation of the liver, heart and surrounding tissues; and anemia. This form of arthritis affects only 10 percent of the population.

Baclofen: a muscle relaxant medication to loosen muscles so they are not so spastic.

Benign: a term to describe non-cancerous tumors or fluids, which tend to grow slowly and do not spread.

Biopsy: removing a sample piece of a tumor, lump, or organ to test to determine what is wrong and if it contains cancerous cells.

Blood count: blood is made up of red and white blood cells. Red blood cells carry oxygen throughout the body. White blood cells defend the body against germs that can cause illness. Blood tests count how many of each type a person has. If the person is ill, the blood counts will be outside the normal amounts.

Blood pressure: the rate at which the heart pumps blood through the body. If blood pressure is too high or too low, it can lead to problems.

Bone marrow: the soft, spongy tissue found inside bones.

Bone marrow transplant: the transfusion of healthy bone marrow cells, taken from a healthy donor, and infused into a person after his or her own unhealthy bone marrow has been removed.

CAT scan/CT scan: pictures of the inside of the body, similar to an x-ray, but with more detail.

Cancer: a disease where the body makes cells that are not normal, which can spread quickly and take over the normal cells if left untreated. There are many different types of cancer.

Catheter: a tube that is surgically implanted into the body, typically under the skin and usually in the large blood vessels of the chest, allowing for drainage of fluids, injection of medicines, or accessibility for surgical instruments. It prevents the need for numerous needle sticks during treatment.

Cerebral palsy: a lifelong condition that affects the communication between the brain and the muscles, causing uncoordinated movement. It results when there is a lack of oxygen to the brain.

Chemotherapy/Chemo: special medicines that treat cancer by attempting to kill cancer cells. It is so strong that it kills both cancer cells and healthy cells, so the medicine has to be carefully controlled so it doesn't damage too many good cells and organs. People getting chemotherapy often lose their hair because of cell damage.

Child Life specialist: a specially trained hospital staff person who helps kids learn about and adjust to illnesses, often through play activities, relaxation, and pain management skills. The specialist works with the entire family and sometimes will go to the child's school to explain the child's illness to classmates.

Denys-Drash syndrome: a disorder with three main parts: kidney disease present at birth, Wilms' tumor (a kidney cancer), and malformation of the reproductive organs.

Diabetes: a disease in which the body does not produce or properly use insulin. Insulin is needed to convert sugar, starches, and other food into energy for daily life. People who have type-1 diabetes must take daily insulin injections.

Dialysis: the use of a special machine that removes waste and additional fluid from the blood, and takes the place of missing or damaged kidneys.

Eczema: a condition when the skin is super itchy and dry.

Evans' syndrome: a rare disease in which a person's antibodies attack his or her own red and white blood cells and platelets, so these cells cannot do their job in the body.

Ewing's sarcoma: a rare disease in which cancer cells are found in the bone or in soft tissue.

Factor: a protein in blood that allows it to clot. Factor is missing from individuals who have blood disorders, such as hemophilia.

Hemiplegia: the condition where a vertical half of a patient's body is weak or paralyzed. For example, an arm and leg on the same side of the body do not function properly.

Hemoglobin: the iron-containing pigment in red blood cells that moves oxygen from the lungs to the cells in all parts of the body.

Hemophilia: an inherited bleeding disorder that prevents the blood from clotting properly due to low levels or the absence of factor, a blood protein. There are mild, moderate, and severe levels of hemophilia, depending on the level of factor in the blood.

HIV: the human immunodeficiency virus that infects and destroys cells of the body's immune system (also called the AIDS virus).

Hodgkin's disease: a type of lymphoma, a cancer in the lymphatic system. The disease causes the cells in the lymphatic system to abnormally reproduce, making the body less able to fight infection.

Hospice: a national organization that offers care to patients and families facing a terminal illness. Hospice care is often provided in the patient's home.

Immune system: the white blood cells and lymph nodes that help protect the body from disease. When a person is sick, the immune system isn't working properly.

Intrathecal baclofen pump: baclofen is a muscle relaxant medication. The baclofen pump system delivers medicine directly into the spinal fluid (intrathecal).

Ischemic anoxic brain injury: occurs when brain cells are deprived of oxygen, which is critical to their survival.

Juvenile rheumatoid arthritis (*see also* Arthritis): a form of arthritis in children ages 16 or younger that causes inflammation and stiffness of the joints.

Kidneys: a pair of internal organs that filter waste materials out of the blood. Kidneys produce important hormones and regulate blood pressure and the levels of water, salt, and minerals in the body.

Leukemia: a cancer of the blood resulting from the abnormal increase in the number of white blood cells. Acute lymphoblastic leukemia (ALL) is a rapidly progressing cancer in which too many lymphocytes, a type of white blood cell, are found in the bone marrow, blood, spleen, liver, and other organs. Acute myelogenous leukemia (AML) is cancer in which too many granulocytes, a type of white blood cell, are found in the bone marrow and blood.

Lymph nodes: tissue or small bumps in the body, usually not felt unless they become swollen. They are like filters that remove germs that can harm the body.

Lymphoma: a type of cancer involving cells of the immune system.

Magnetic resonance imaging (MRI): a diagnostic procedure that produces detailed images of organs and structures within the body.

Malignant: a term used to describe cancerous tumors that tend to grow rapidly and invade and destroy nearby healthy tissue.

Medulloblastoma: malignant tumors formed from poorly developed cells at a very early stage of life, which develop in the cerebellum part of the brain.

Multiple sclerosis (MS): a chronic, inflammatory disease that affects the central nervous system. MS symptoms may include changes in sensation, visual problems, muscle weakness, depression, difficulties with coordination and speech, severe fatigue, and pain.

Muscular dystrophy (Duchenne): an inherited disorder characterized by rapidly progressive muscle weakness that starts in the legs and later affects the whole body. Most people who have this disease die by the age of 25.

Myelodysplastic syndrome (MDS): formerly known as pre-leukemia, it's a collection of blood conditions resulting from ineffective production of blood cells. May lead to acute myelogenous leukemia.

Nephritic syndrome: a collection of symptoms associated with disorders affecting the kidneys.

Neutropenic: a really low white blood cell count that makes a person prone to having fevers or getting sick because the white blood cells are not fighting off illness. It can be a side effect of chemotherapy treatments.

Oncologist: a doctor who specializes in treating patients with cancer.

Orthopedist: a doctor who specializes in the skeletal structure of the human body.

Osteosarcoma: a cancer that affects bones, and is generally found in children and teens.

Platelets: cells in the blood that help the blood clot when a person is bleeding.

Port: a tube (a Hickman or Broviac catheter) that is surgically implanted into the body, typically under the skin and usually in the large blood vessels of the chest, allowing for drainage of fluids, injection of medicines, or accessibility for surgical instruments. It prevents the need for numerous needle sticks during treatment.

Post-transplant lymphoproliferative disorder (PTLD): a group of B cell (related to the immune system) lymphomas (a type of cancer) occurring in patients following organ transplant. It is a rare condition occurring in 0.2 percent of patients within one year of a transplant.

Radiation therapy: a treatment where high-energy rays are used to kill or shrink cancer cells. The rays place radioactive materials directly in the tumor.

Red blood cells: the most common type of blood cell in the body, and the means of delivering oxygen from the lungs to body tissues via the blood. Red blood cells also carry carbon dioxide back to the lungs so it can be exhaled. If the red blood count is low, the body may not be getting the oxygen it needs. If the count is too high, there is a chance that the red blood cells will clump together and block tiny blood vessels, making it hard for the red blood cells to carry oxygen.

Relapse: when cancer reappears after a period of being cancer-free.

Remission: complete or partial disappearance of the signs and symptoms of cancer in response to treatment. It may not be a cure, but the disease is under control.

Rheumatoid arthritis: a chronic disease with pain, stiffness, swelling, and sometimes destruction of the joints.

Sarcoma: a malignant tumor growing from connective tissues such as cartilage, fat, muscle, or bone.

Seizure: abnormal electrical activity in the brain typically causing a person's body to shake uncontrollably. There are different types of seizures and different levels of severity. Usually, the person doesn't have any memory of what happened during a seizure.

Shunt: a connecting tube to allow fluid to flow between two locations within the body.

Sickle cell anemia: a disease where a person inherits two abnormal genes (one from each parent) that causes the red blood cells to change shape. Instead of being flexible and round, the red blood cells are more rigid and curved (like a crescent moon) in the shape of a "sickle," a farm tool. Since sickle cells don't move through the bloodstream easily, they can clog blood vessels and deprive the body's tissues and organs of oxygen. Though this is a disease that mostly affects people of African descent, it also affects people in other ethnic groups, including people of Mediterranean and Middle Eastern descent. There is no known cure for this painful disease.

Sickle cell crisis: the pain that occurs when the flow of blood is blocked because the sickle cells are stuck in a blood vessel. This can occur when an individual experiences sudden and extreme temperature changes, such as leaving an air conditioned building and going outside where it is very hot, or even jumping into a cold pool.

Spina bifida: a disorder from incomplete development of the brain, spinal cord, and/or their protective coverings, caused by the failure of the unborn baby's spine to close properly. The resulting damage is varying degrees of paralysis of the lower limbs, which is permanent.

Spinal cord: a bundle of nerves along the backbone that carries messages between the brain and the rest of the body.

Spinal tap: a medical procedure where a doctor uses a long needle to take a sample of the fluid around the spinal cord. This test is used to diagnose certain illness, such as meningitis and different types of cancer.

Staph infection: an infection in the body resulting from bacteria on the skin entering the body through an open cut.

Tethered cord syndrome: normally, the spinal cord is able to move freely when an individual bends or stretches, but when the spinal cord is tethered, it cannot move freely and puts tension on the spinal cord. This occurs when an individual is born with spina bifida.

Tumor: an abnormal mass or lump of tissue. Tumors can be benign (not cancerous) or malignant (cancerous).

White blood cells: cells of the immune system that defend the body against infectious disease and foreign materials by attacking and destroying the bacteria, virus, or other organism causing infection. White blood cells are about 1 percent of the blood in a healthy person, but when a person has an infection, the number of white cells rises very quickly. A white blood cell count is often used to determine if there is an infection or to see how the body is dealing with cancer treatments.

X-ray: a diagnostic test that uses invisible electromagnetic energy beams to produce images on film of internal tissues, bones, and organs.

About the Authors

Axel Dahlberg

Axel Dahlberg holds an M.F.A. degree in creative writing and taught writing at Arizona State University. Axel has been writing ever since he could hold a crayon, initially on walls, furniture, and patient animals. He knew he had found his calling when he heard those first encouraging words from Miss Rich, his first-grade teacher, who said, "This is good." He has never looked back.

Janis Russell Love

Janis has been a successful entrepreneur for 26 years, initially starting a staffing company in the male-dominated industry of computer technology. She was successful because of her ability to find "purple squirrels," hard-to-find computer-types with rare skill sets. This ability, perhaps more than any other, proved critical in interviewing ill children who, understandably, were closely guarded and often not excited to speak into a tape recorder.

Photos courtesy of Mary McAlister, Phoenix, Arizona

Other Great Books from Free Spirit!

When Nothing Matters Anymore
A Survival Guide for Depressed Teens
by Bev Cobain, R.N.,C.
Written for teens with depression—and those who feel despondent, dejected, or alone—this powerful book offers help, hope, and potentially life-saving facts and advice. Includes true stories from teens who have dealt with depression, survival tips, resources, and more.
For ages 13 & up. $14.95, 176 pp., illust., softcover, 6" x 9"

Too Stressed to Think?
A Teen Guide to Staying Sane When Life Makes You Crazy
by Annie Fox, M.Ed., and Ruth Kirschner
When stress has the "survival brain" on overdrive, what happens to the "thinking brain"? How can teens stay cool and make smart choices when the pressure's on? This book is packed with stress-lessening tools teens can use every day. Scenarios describe situations readers can relate to. Each is followed by a process for reducing or stopping the stress and making sound decisions. Quotes from real teens remind stressed-out readers that they're not alone. Includes resources.
For ages 12 & up. $14.95, 176 pp., 2-color illust., softcover, 6" x 9"

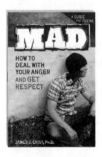

Mad
How to Deal with Your Anger and Get Respect
by James J. Crist, Ph.D.
Feeling mad is a normal human emotion. But some teens go too far and get into trouble with their parents, in school, or the law. Their anger controls them and affects their lives in negative, sometimes long-lasting ways. This practical, supportive book helps teens learn whether they have an anger problem, why we get angry, and how anger affects our bodies and relationships. Practical tools and strategies help them control their anger and avoid poor decisions and actions; insights from real teens let them know they're not alone. The final chapters explore mental health problems that can complicate anger management and the role of counseling and psychotherapy. Includes resources. *For ages 13 & up. $13.95, 160 pp., 2-color, illust., softcover, 6" x 9"*

What to Do When You're Sad & Lonely
A Guide for Kids
by James J. Crist, Ph.D.
Everyone feels sad and lonely sometimes. Growing numbers of children suffer from depression, a disease often mistaken for sadness. Written by a psychologist, this book helps kids deal with painful feelings. The first part presents coping skills ("Blues Busters") kids can learn and practice on their own. The second part focuses on grief, depression, Bipolar Disorder, and other problems too big for kids to handle and describes what it's like to go to counseling. For ages 9–13.
$9.95, 128 pp., 2-color, illust., softcover, 5⅜" x 8⅜"

After You Lose Someone You Love
Advice and Insight from the Diaries of Three Kids Who've Been There
as told by Amy, Allie, and David Dennison, foreword by Harold S. Kushner
"This is a journal about what happened to us.... One night, Dad just died and that was that."
Twins Amy and Allie were eight years old and their brother David was four when their beloved
father died suddenly in his sleep. Their real-life account is an honest, insightful, and deeply
moving perspective on death, its aftermath, and the journey through grief and growth.
For all ages. $9.95, 128 pp., B&W photos & illust., softcover, 5⅜" x 8⅜"

When a Friend Dies
A Book for Teens About Grieving & Healing (Revised & Updated Edition)
by Marilyn E. Gootman, Ed.D., foreword by R.E.M. lead singer Michael Stipe
The death of a friend is a wrenching event for anyone at any age. Teenagers especially need help
coping with this painful loss. This sensitive book answers questions grieving teens often have,
like "How should I be acting?" "Is it wrong to go to parties and have fun?" and "What if I can't
handle my grief on my own?" The advice is gentle, non-preachy, and compassionate. The revised
edition includes new quotes from teens, new resources, and new insights into losing a friend
through violence. Also recommended for parents and teachers of teens who have experienced a
painful loss. For ages 11 & up. $9.95, 128 pp., B&W photos, softcover, 5" x 7"

Fighting Invisible Tigers
Stress Management for Teens (Revised & Updated Third Edition)
by Earl Hipp
While eliminating stress from life isn't realistic, young people can learn to control how they
respond to it. This book offers proven techniques that teens can use to deal with stressful situations in school, at home, and among friends, including assertiveness, positive self-talk, time
management, relaxation exercises, and much more. Filled with interesting facts, student quotes,
and fun activities, this book is a great resource for any teen who's said, "I'm stressed out!" For
ages 11 & up. $14.95, 160 pp., 2-color, illust., softcover, 6" x 9"

*To place an order or to request a free catalog of Self-Help for Kids® and
Self-Help for Teens® materials, please write, call, email, or visit our Web site:*

Free Spirit Publishing Inc.
217 Fifth Avenue North • Suite 200 • Minneapolis, MN 55401-1299
toll-free 800.735.7323 • local 612.338.2068 • fax 612.337.5050
help4kids@freespirit.com • www.freespirit.com

Fast, Friendly, and Easy to Use

www.freespirit.com

Browse the catalog

Info & extras

Many ways to search

Quick check-out

Stop in and see!

Our Web site makes it easy to find the positive, reliable resources you need to empower teens and kids of all ages.

The Catalog.
Start browsing with just one click.

Beyond the Home Page.
Information and extras such as links and downloads.

The Search Box.
Find anything superfast.

Your Voice.
See testimonials from customers like you.

Request the Catalog.
Browse our catalog on paper, too!

The Nitty-Gritty.
Toll-free numbers, online ordering information, and more.

The 411.
News, reviews, awards, and special events.

 Our Web site is a secure commerce site. All of the personal information you enter at our site—including your name, address, and credit card number—is secure. So you can order with confidence when you order online from Free Spirit!

For a fast and easy way to receive our practical tips, helpful information, and special offers, send your email address to upbeatnews@freespirit.com. View a sample letter and our privacy policy at www.freespirit.com.

1.800.735.7323 • fax 612.337.5050 • help4kids@freespirit.com

Ideas, Doodles, Wishes, & Goals, Ideas, Doodles, Wishes & Goals